GHOST STORIES
of FLORIDA

Dan Asfar

LONE
PINE

Lone Pine Publishing International

© 2005 by Lone Pine Publishing International, Inc.
First printed in 2005 10 9 8 7 6 5 4 3 2 1
Printed in Canada

The Publisher: Lone Pine Publishing International

Distributed by Lone Pine Publishing
1808 B Street NW, Suite 140
Auburn, WA 98001
USA

Websites: www.lonepinepublishing.com
www.ghostbooks.net

National Library of Canada Cataloguing in Publication Data

Asfar, Dan, 1973-
Ghost stories of Florida / Dan Asfar.

ISBN-13: 978-1-894877-22-0
ISBN-10: 1-894877-22-5

1. Ghosts--Florida. I. Title.

GR110.F5A84 2005   133.1'09759   C2005-903771-7

Photo Credits: Every effort has been made to accurately credit sources. Any errors or omissions should be directed to the publisher for changes in future editions. The images in this book are reproduced by the kind permission of the following sources: Biltmore Hotel (p. 146); Istock (pp. 4–5: Sue Ding; p. 36: Stefani Greene; p.43: Sandra O'Claire; p. 47: Cathy Kaplan; p. 57: Jonas Engstrom; p. 123: Rhonda Roberts); Library of Congress (p. 50: USZ62-125405; p. 170: D4-17494; p 179: HABS, FLA,55-SAUG,1-14; p. 183: HABS, FLA,55-SAUG,1-39).

The stories, folklore and legends in this book are based on the author's collection of sources including individuals whose experiences have led them to believe they have encountered phenomena of some kind or another. They are meant to entertain, and neither the publisher nor the author claims these stories represent fact.

PC: P5

For Raùl and Rosa

Contents

Chapter 1: Ghostly Folklore

Chapter 2: Haunted Houses

Chapter 3: Haunted Landscapes

Chapter 4: Haunted Businesses

Chapter 5: Ghosts in Public Places

Acknowledgments

While many would insist that ghost stories spring from the province of the imagination, it should be stated here that none of the tales in this book are the author's creation. All are based either on established folklore or testimonials from individuals who claim to have come face-to-face with supernatural entities. For the folklore, the author must acknowledge those published raconteurs whose work has inspired and informed a number of the following stories. Thanks go to Jack Powell, author of *Haunting Sunshine* (2001), Kim Cool, for *Ghost Stories of Sarasota* (2003), Joyce Elson Moore, who wrote the *Haunt Hunter's Guide to Florida* (1998) and Dave Lapham, for *Ghosts of St. Augustine* (1997). And for the firsthand accounts, thanks to all those who were willing to speak about their experiences. This book would not have been possible without your help.

Introduction

Ghosts have been around for as long as people have been telling stories. Homer's *Iliad*, one of the earliest narratives of Western civilization, has the spirit of the recently slain Patroclus appearing before Achilles to warn the legendary warrior of his own demise. Almost 2000 years later, everyone's favorite playwright, William Shakespeare, brought Banquo back from the dead to torture the conscience of the guilt-ridden Macbeth. Today, movie theaters across the country screen a steady stream of films that feature the restless dead and their unnerving habit of tormenting the living.

There's no arguing that the dead have always occupied a big place in cultural expression. The inevitability of death and the question of what follows are fundamental to the human condition, and all societies across the globe have their own ways of approaching it. Cultures near and far, remote and cosmopolitan, might be partly understood by the way their religious beliefs and folkloric narratives tackle the notion of the great hereafter.

Not to worry. The following pages do not endeavor to take on such heavy topic matter. It's a book of ghost stories, after all, and it probably goes without saying that the reader didn't pick it up with hopes of coming to grips with such questions. Yet it must be stated that not one of these tales has hatched from the whimsy of the author's imagination. All of these stories are said to be true—they are supernatural accounts told by Floridians, ghostly folklore that has survived the centuries. Some of them are well known, others are more obscure, and each and every one of them are purported to find their roots in fact rather than fiction. These are Florida's ghost stories; the author can only claim to be a faithful chronicler of some of the haunts in its history, the uncanny experiences of its citizens. It is up to the readers to decide whether or not to believe.

1
Ghostly Folklore

The Gamble Place

"Damned little beasts!" Rollie Johnson was heard shouting from the end of the bar. "One of these nights they're gonna kill me, making me chase them up and down Spruce Creek all night long." Rollie was drunk again and, as was usually the case when he'd thrown back a few too many, he found himself entertaining a big group of smiling faces.

"You bet, Rollie," the man next to him laughed. "Men your age shouldn't be asked to spend every Halloween runnin' around in the dark, lookin' for..." The man paused, waiting for the word he had heard Rollie spit out every first of November for as far back as he could remember. "What'cha call'em again?"

"Gnomes," Rollie grunted, sinking his head into his hands. "Blasted gnomes."

"That's right," the man continued. "Gnomes—sounds like they're quick on their feet. Maybe it's time to let a greener lad take over at the Gamble Place."

"I'll take care of the grove!" one of the younger men at the bar piped up. "Little guys wouldn't know what hit 'em!"

The crowd surrounding miserable Rollie Johnson erupted in laughter. No one except kids and fools believed Rollie's story about the gnomes. He'd been complaining about the "damned little beasts" for 20-some years, ever since he'd worked as the caretaker of James Gamble's five-acre citrus grove in 1907. On the first day of every November, an exhausted Rollie Johnson could be counted on to come into town, swearing a blue streak about the gnomes he'd been chasing around all night. And from the very beginning, everyone assumed it was just another one of Rollie's grand old larks.

Rollie was one of Daytona Beach's more gregarious personalities. Fond of tall tales and big laughs, he was never without a ridiculous story about some impossible adventure out on the Gamble plantation. While kids always listened in wide-eyed wonder, not too many adults took him seriously. "That's just Rollie," they'd say, "always playing to a crowd." Though Rollie would eventually fess up about whatever absurdity he'd invented before heading back to his place on the Gamble property, he never once took back a word about the gnomes.

James Gamble was the same Cincinnati tycoon who made up one half of Proctor & Gamble, the world-famous soap company. It is said that Gamble was the first northerner to make a winter home in Florida. After discovering the land near Daytona Beach on a fishing trip, Gamble bought the 150-acre plot in 1898, which included the orange grove that Rollie Johnson would eventually be hired to take care of.

Rollie lived at the Gamble Place, watching over the property when the Gambles were out of town, about 10 months out of the year, from March to late December. In addition to looking after the five acres of oranges, Rollie's duties included general maintenance of the grounds. He was a sturdy, if slightly dissolute man, and never had an issue with any part of his work—except, that is, the gnomes. No one had told him about the gnomes.

He would never know where the gnomes came from, or whose idea it was to put them there, but Rollie always thought there was something strange about the little stone statues scattered around the grounds. From the beginning, the small pointy-capped figures—whether depicted as industrious workers or idle loafers—seemed a bit too lifelike for Rollie's comfort. It wasn't so much about sculptural skill; with their rough stone visages and sightless gazes, there were no Michelangelo masterpieces planted in the Gamble Place. No. They didn't *look* too lifelike. It was something Rollie couldn't put his finger on. There was a *feeling* he got when he walked among the still figures: a feeling that he wasn't alone. The gnomes' smiling stone eyes were somehow watching him—and laughing.

For much of the first year, Rollie convinced himself that he was spending too much time on his own, did his best to ignore the feeling and continued on with his work. That was before his first Halloween. We can only guess what his initial reaction was that October night, when the darkness suddenly came to life with strange whispers and chuckles, and all around, the sound of tiny feet running to and fro. We do know what thought struck him when the light of his lantern revealed his first gnome bolting through the greenery: *Tarnation! If Mr. Gamble finds out that I let his gnomes get away, I'll get fired darn straight!*

And so began Rollie Johnson's yearly tradition of chasing gnomes through the darkness. Every Halloween, Gamble's stone statues came to life, and Rollie, lantern in hand, spent the whole night running back and forth through the orange grove, tracking down one gnome at a time. They were fast, no doubt, and smart, but their short legs proved to be a serious disadvantage, and though it was hard work, Rollie was always able to catch all of them before the sun came up. He'd catch them one by one and, much to the groundskeeper's relief, the gnomes struggled only for a few seconds before transforming back into stone statues for another 364 days. Only after each and every gnome was back where it belonged did Rollie head back into Daytona Beach, spreading word of the incredible night to everyone he met along the way.

Needless to say, the first few Halloweens left him stunned and more than a little frightened. But somewhere between his third and fourth year, the nocturnal hunt began to feel less like a mystery and more like a pain in the butt. And it only got worse as he got older. The gnomes remained as spry and energetic as they'd been the first time they'd sprung from stone, but Rollie's speed and reflexes succumbed to the years. Each passing Halloween saw his hunt extend deeper into the night, and to numb the aches in his ever-stiffening joints, he took to supplementing his chases with ever-increasing amounts of whiskey. Sore, angry and drunk, Rollie was always a sight to see stumbling into town on November 1st. The bad humor of his later years took nothing away from his popularity in Daytona Beach.

Rollie Johnson died in 1934, insisting to the end that there really were gnomes at the Gamble Place, and to the end, all who knew him assumed that this was just Rollie being Rollie—a showman to his last breath. But the people of Daytona were mistaken if they believed they would hear nothing more of little people at the Gamble Place. In fact, things were just getting started.

Given Rollie's lifelong frustration with undersized men in pointy hats, it's likely he would have been shocked by the fate of the land he'd once tended. The scheme was born from the imagination of Gamble's son-in-law, Judge Nippert. It was 1937, years after Gamble passed away, when the Walt Disney production *Snow White* was released in theaters across the United States. The world's first full-length animated movie featured in full color, *Snow White* was a massive success, loved by kids and parents.

Nippert, especially taken with the movie, came upon an idea while visiting his late father-in-law's Florida plantation. It occurred to him while he was looking at the stone gnomes positioned around the grounds: why not create a life-size environment replicating the dwarves' house? Kids who loved *Snow White* could come to visit real versions of the buildings they saw on screen. Within three months, the fantastical little park was complete. Thrilled fans could walk through the dwarves' home and see the same large fireplace from the movie and, upstairs, seven miniature beds with the names of their mythical owners carved into the headboards. Not far away, nestled among the trees, was a witch's hut, along with the movie's wishing well and dwarves' mine.

Aiming only to put together a quaint, little getaway for families, Nippert had no idea how big his theme park idea was going to get. Word spread, and Walt Disney himself visited in 1938. It was said that he was so impressed that he commissioned life-size dolls of the characters to be made and sent to the seven dwarves' Florida home.

It is impossible to say what the gnomes thought of their new visitors, but as it turned out, they didn't have to share their home for too long—well, not too long in gnome years, anyway. Seventeen years later, Walt Disney opened *Disneyland* in California, and the dwarves' humble little abode was quickly overshadowed by the world's biggest theme park, which may or may not have been inspired by Nippert's operation.

As for Rollie Johnson and his accursed gnomes, since the groundskeeper's passing, there have been no accounts of little people making mischief in the small hours. Years have passed, and many of the gnomes, while still there, have been worn by the seasons, their moss-covered features chipped and broken. That's not to say that there haven't been strange stories circulating about the old plantation. Donated to the Nature Conservancy in 1983, the Gamble Place was closed to the public for many years, and was reopened to the public in 2005.

Every now and then, you hear a story about someone who knows someone who claims to have seen a light swinging back and forth around the old Gamble house. In some versions, the witnesses are spooked by the sight of the solitary light bobbing in the dark, and they leave without taking a closer look. Other times, people have been a little more adventurous, sneaking forward until they are close enough to see that there is nothing attached to the light: a disembodied illumination, jerking to and fro as though attached to an invisible chain, and moving erratically over the grounds. But an even smaller number of people, still more intrigued than frightened, have continued forward to get a closer look. It is these intrepid few who have heard it. The voice. Every time, it is described the same way: the voice of an old man, always tired and angry, always grumbling and cursing something about gnomes under his breath.

Another case of urban legends translating old folktales? Playful teenagers making up stories for fun? Overactive imaginations, convinced they have seen what isn't there? Or maybe, just maybe, the spirit of Rollie Johnson, still groaning and swearing and chasing gnomes around until the sun rises on November 1st? Well, if he is still chasing the little guys around, to his credit, all the statues are still there, most of them old and weatherworn—except for a small few that are suspiciously unscathed, without a shred of moss growing over them, but expressing a strange twinkle in their gray, otherwise lifeless faces.

The Headless Rider of Seahorse Key

Pierre LeBlanc sat atop his palomino stallion, looking out at the waters of the Gulf of Mexico stretching endlessly before him, cursing to himself because there was no one else around. "'Ere's to prayin' ya grow barnacles on yer backside and dey 'ave to cut 'em out with a dull blade," the irate Frenchman muttered into the wind. "'Ere's to prayin' that the wounds rot and dey 'ave to cut 'em again." LeBlanc spat on the ground and guided his horse away from the edge of the rocky promontory, down to the beach below.

"At least 'e left me with a horse, the scurvy dog," he said.

And a fine horse it was. The palomino under LeBlanc was a gorgeous animal, with a flowing white mane and tail, and a brilliant coat that shone golden brown under the clear blue sky. "Looks like it's just you an' me," LeBlanc said, leaning down and patting his horse on the neck. "I suppose I oughtta come up with a name for ye."

Several hours later, LeBlanc was sitting on the beach, cooking a fish he'd just caught over a small fire. His horse still didn't have a name, and LeBlanc had given up trying to come up with one. His thoughts were distracted as he gazed past the surf in silence, straining his vision in vain for some sign of the city he loved. He took a swig from the bottle of rum at his side, dwelling bitterly on the revelry he knew he'd be missing. He closed his eyes and imagined the sight of New Orleans appearing out of the darkness, its reflections of light dancing on the black water. The waterfront chaos made it his favorite place in the world—the rude laughter spilling out of the taverns, the raucous music, the women of easy leisure.

LeBlanc opened his eyes to the sizzling fish and the deserted beach. "Two cursed months at sea, and this is the reward I get."

And then he froze. He didn't so much hear it as sense it—he wasn't alone. Someone was approaching on the sand behind him, close. The realization made his hand creep towards the cutlass that was tucked into his belt.

"Could be worse," came a stranger's voice, "at least ye've got plenty of rum to pass the—"

The man's words were cut short by the point of LeBlanc's weapon, which now hovered a hair's breadth away from the man's throat. "Aye, plenty of rum indeed," LeBlanc growled, acknowledging the small mountain of bottles his shipmates left behind, "and plenty of time ta pass as well. Though I don't plan on sharin' either of 'em with anyone."

The man was dressed in loose, sun-bleached clothing. A sack overflowing with snake skins hung from his shoulder; a rifle was slung across his back and he had a pistol tucked into the sash around his waist. It occurred to LeBlanc that this man, if he had wanted, could have shot him while his back was turned. "Easy, friend," the man said, raising his hands cautiously. "Didn't mean to sneak up on ya."

"What the hell are you doin' on this godforsaken island?" LeBlanc shot back, his sword unwavering.

"Hunting snakes," the worried man replied. "Skins are worth a handsome penny on the mainland." He nodded at the sack stuffed full of snakeskin. "My boat's just past them trees. If you're stranded, I can pilot ye back first light."

LeBlanc considered the man's words. He noted, to his satisfaction, that his visitor definitely looked frightened. "Snake hunter, eh?" LeBlanc grunted, lowering his cutlass slightly. "Looks about right, though I'd just as soon take you for a grand flea-ridden rat."

A smile spread across the man's face. "It's that bad, is it? I've been out on this island fer weeks now, I reckon. I'll be glad to be back on the mainland."

LeBlanc jammed his cutlass back into his belt and sat back down next to his bottle of rum. "Yer not the only one."

The man sat down slowly as well. "And what misfortune brought ye to this rock, with no vessel but a horse and a king's ransom in rum?"

"My misfortune ain't none of yer business," LeBlanc snapped back, a venomous look in his eye.

"If you say so," the man muttered, moving to stand up. "I'll get back to the snakes, then. Better company."

LeBlanc stared sullenly at the fire as the man got to his feet and began to walk away. He thought about the coming night that stretched out before him and all the days before the ship returned, a nameless palomino his only company. A moment passed before LeBlanc called out. "Hoy there!" he said, "don't snake hunters drink rum?"

The man stopped in his tracks, turned slowly. "Funny you should ask," the man said with a smile. "I was just wonderin' whether or not I should shoot ye for them bottles."

LeBlanc laughed. "Sit down! Have one then. Best to keep a thirsty rat and his guns where I can see 'em."

The snake hunter didn't need to be cajoled. He walked back to where LeBlanc was sitting, a conciliatory grin on his bristled face. Falling onto the beach, he caught the bottle LeBlanc tossed at him, popped the cork and took a healthy swig. He wiped his mouth with the back of his hand and stared appreciatively at the bottle. "Too much time chasin' snakes through the trees. Almost forgot what civilization tasted like."

LeBlanc snorted. "I don't care even a little for civilization. New Orleans is the place I'm missin'."

The man looked at LeBlanc closely then. "New Orleans, is it? Too much mayhem in that port for my taste. Pirates comin' out of the walls. I heard say that Jean Laffite's on his way there right now. I'd hate to be on the waterfront when that ship anchors."

A grinning LeBlanc threw back what was left in his bottle. He reached for another. "That a fact? What quarrel could a snake hunter 'ave with Laffite?"

"No quarrel," the man quickly responded, taking a big swig of rum. "Never even met the Terror of the Gulf, and that's the way I want to keep it."

LeBlanc's smile widened. "The Terror of the Gulf," he said to himself. "Is that what they call 'im now."

"Though I wouldn't complain none if I stumbled on some of his gold one day."

If the man noticed the suddenly serious expression on LeBlanc's face, he gave no indication. "They say there's a fortune in booty buried on these islands."

"Bah!" LeBlanc shot back. "Children's stories. What fools actually believe those lies about pirates and their buried treasure?" He took a swig from his bottle and pulled a knife from his boot, viciously stabbing at the fish cooking over the fire. He took a big bite out of the fish and washed it down with another mouthful of rum, not noticing the snake hunter move the bottle behind his back and pour half the bottle onto the sand.

"I guess you're right," the man said, quickly moving the bottle back to his lap. "Nothing but bedtime stories for the kids. Well, here's to bedtime stories." The man raised his bottle.

"That's more like it," LeBlanc grumbled, raising his own bottle and downing the rest of it in one huge gulp. Again, he didn't notice the snake hunter pour his own rum into the sand.

"Buried treasure or no," the man said as LeBlanc raised an unsteady arm for another bottle. "You sure as hell drink like a pirate."

"Pirate you say," the now-drunk LeBlanc's lazy gaze moved from his drinking partner to the fish skewered on the end of his knife. "Arrr…I'm no pirate, fool. I catch fish for a living!" LeBlanc burst into a long fit of ugly laughter, and the snake hunter joined in, though there was no mirth in his eyes.

"A fisherman indeed," the man said, pouring the last of his rum into the sand and opening another bottle. "You're pretty fast with a cutlass for a fisherman!"

LeBlanc leapt to his feet then, yanking his weapon from his belt. "Make no mistake!" he hollered, raining vicious blows on invisible enemies. "I've gutted a good many fish in my day!" Stumbling over his feet with an overextended thrust, he fell flat onto the beach in a drunken heap, laughing hysterically.

If he had even half his wits about him, he'd have noticed that the snake hunter had emptied his second bottle onto the ground, while still reaching for a third. He goaded LeBlanc to keep drinking, and the drunken Frenchman continued to throw back the rum. By this time, he was beyond drunk. Details were beyond him. He didn't notice that the snake hunter was speaking far too steadily to have drunk the three empty bottles lying in front of him. Neither did he notice that the man's questions were becoming inquisitive enough to be suspicious. And his own answers were inconsistent enough to warrant suspicion.

LeBlanc claimed to be a fisherman who'd been stranded on the island after his ship took in too much water. When the snake hunter offered to take him off the island the next day, LeBlanc became a trader sight-seeing on the little gulf island until his ship came by to pick him up. What was he trading? The first time the snake hunter asked, LeBlanc was a horse trader, the second time, rum.

And then, when LeBlanc had drunk enough to drown three normal men, he lurched to his feet and informed the all-too-sober man next to him that it was time he retired. "Time for sleep, rat," LeBlanc slurred through half-closed eyes. "Don't touch them bottles."

And with that, the Frenchman grabbed his palomino's reins and staggered down the beach, unaware that the snake hunter was cautiously following behind. LeBlanc turned off the beach into the trees before a cluster of boulders. The snake hunter was careful in the woods, choosing his steps carefully so as not to give himself away. He needn't have worried, though; LeBlanc was muttering loudly to himself as he stumbled through to another, smaller stretch of sand, hidden from the rest of the beach by a cluster of rocks and boulders on either side.

"Damn ye Lafitte," the drunken man said, staggering to a hammock he had tied between two trees. "Damn ye and yer stinkin' booty, leavin' me here to guard it with a horse and a rat filth snake hunter." LeBlanc threw himself onto the hammock but landed unbalanced and was dumped unceremoniously onto the ground. Roaring in frustration, he pounded the beach with his fist and yelled at the night's sky. "I want New Orleans!"

The snake hunter, hidden in the cover of the trees, was watching intently, an urgent gleam in his eyes. His suspicions had been correct. *Booty. LeBlanc was a pirate, and there was treasure on this island.* He let out a little gasp when his eyes fell on the pile of loose sand a few feet from where LeBlanc's hammock was strung up, a shovel protruding from the freshly covered pit. *It was right there! Pirate's treasure!*

• • •

LeBlanc had no way of knowing how much time had passed when he came to, but the sky was still dark, and the world was still spinning through his liquor-addled vision. Too pained even to groan, he rolled over onto his back, wiped the sand and spittle from his face and kneaded his aching forehead in his hands. Still drunk,

LeBlanc was utterly confused. *Rocks. Sand. Water. Where am I? And why?*

Then, awareness began to cut through his drunken fog. Memories were returning, one at a time. *Bound for New Orleans, when Jean Lafitte ordered me to watch over booty they'd taken from an English vessel. The rum. The horse. The snake hunter.* No sooner had he recalled the man he'd shared rum with that it struck him that something was wrong. *What was that sound?*

He sat up slowly, rubbing his eyes and staring into the darkness. There was a man there, lifting something out of a freshly dug pit, something big. A chest. Then it hit him with all the force of a thundering typhoon: *The treasure! He's trying to sneak away with it!*

LeBlanc lifted himself onto two unsteady feet and shouted, "You scurvy-ridden rat! I'll have your liver for lunch!"

The snake hunter spun around just as LeBlanc drew his cutlass and lunged. By all rights, the sight of Pierre LeBlanc bearding down on him, weapon raised, should have been the last thing the snake hunter ever saw. LeBlanc was an experienced swordsman and under normal circumstances would have promptly dealt his death-blow. But these weren't normal circumstances. The French pirate was far too drunk, and wound up tripping over his own feet just before he was about to strike. He fell forward, his cutlass opening a bloody swath across the snake hunter's face.

It was an ugly wound, but not a fatal one, and the snake hunter was able to grab LeBlanc's sword hand after the pirate tumbled into him. The pair grappled, a desperate battle of life and death on the deserted beach. LeBlanc was struggling to give himself enough room to use his cutlass, while the snake hunter held onto the pirate's sword arm for dear life, knowing full well that he would quickly meet his end if he gave LeBlanc enough room to swing his weapon.

LeBlanc was livid, and he kept up a string of ceaseless threats and insults as they struggled. "Son of a wheezing one-eyed mongrel! Putrid mass of bat filth! Treacherous jellyfish! Bottom-feeder! I'll cut you from gill to stinking gill!" Unfortunately for LeBlanc, however, while the excessive alcohol he'd consumed that night may have inspired his ugly epithets, it did nothing for his reflexes, or his coordination. A man he would have bested on any other day was giving him a fight.

When it ended, it ended fast. The snake hunter's grip on LeBlanc's sword hand was still firm when he jutted his leg out behind the pirate and pushed him hard. LeBlanc fell in mid-curse, hitting the beach with a thud, losing his grip on his sword. When he looked up, his opponent was standing over him, cutlass in hand, poised to strike.

"You've lost," the snake hunter gasped, wiping the blood from his face. "Yield, and you'll live to see tomorrow."

LeBlanc didn't say a word but sat up slowly, his lips moving in a wordless litany of rage. "That's right," the snake hunter continued, backing up slowly. "Sit still, and I'll be gone before you know it." The man stopped when he was next to the chest of gold, silver and jewels. He knelt slowly and shoveled a handful into the sack that had been emptied of its snake skins. "I'm not taking all of it," the man said. "Just enough so that I won't have to hunt for no more snakes, understand?"

But if Leblanc understood, it did nothing to kill his hostility. When the snake hunter looked away for an instant, distracted by a big jewel that was shining in the chest, LeBlanc lunged. Pulling his knife from his boot, he jumped forward in one motion, roaring an oath of bloody murder over the sound of the crashing surf.

Again, LeBlanc may have been able to complete his murderous purpose had the rum not taken its toll. He was a step too slow, giving the snake hunter the time he needed. The cutlass swept out in a lethal arc, flashing steel sweeping through the drunken pirate's neck, severing his head clean from its body.

Headless, the body stood still for a dreadful instant before tumbling to the sand next to the gaping face of Pierre LeBlanc. The man standing over the body screamed. The snake hunter may have had no qualms about taking his share of some stolen gold, but he was no murderer, and the sight of the headless body lying in front of him sent a cold panic through him. The island was deserted; there wasn't a soul around to see what he'd done; he would not be judged. But as he stood by the open treasure chest, watching LeBlanc's blood seep into the pit where the booty had been buried, the snake hunter knew beyond any doubt that he'd feel like a fugitive for the rest of his days. He grabbed one more handful of treasure, and without a second look, ran into the woods, dropping LeBlanc's cutlass as he went, leaving the chest of treasure, a nameless palomino and a headless pirate on the beach behind him.

It cannot be said, with any certainty, exactly what the snake hunter did with himself after he murdered Pierre LeBlanc. Were dogs of terror nipping at his heels as he ran from the headless corpse? Did guilt and panic drive him to flee from the scene on his boat that same night? Maybe the only thing he suffered from was an aversion to blood, and after the shock of the decapitation faded, he was able to catch his breath, get some sleep and leave the island at first light, cradling his bag full of ill-gained treasure.

No one is certain what became of the snake hunter. It isn't known whether he lived the rest of his days in money-eyed ease or whether he was forever plagued by what he'd done to come by his riches. Did he tell his story in lit parlors, with zeal and dramatic flourishes? Or in guilt-ridden whispers, half-drunk, to sympathetic ears in darkened drinking rooms? All that can be said for sure is that whenever he did tell his tale, it was only to strangers, and he was always careful to leave out his own name. This made sense, as everyone in the southeastern United States at the time knew of the pirate Jean Laffite, and only a fool would have advertised himself as the person who killed a dreaded outlaw and made away with some of his loot.

This, of course, is where the cynical reader will pipe up. If the snake hunter's name was never revealed, then the entire story could have likely been made up, and then passed on, year after year, from one set of incredulous ears to the next, until it became enshrined in the canon of Florida's folklore. Certainly a valid point, if there was nothing more to the story. But the unsettling stories of Seahorse Key started to circulate. No one knows who saw it first, but it wasn't long afterward that people began to associate the horrible sight on Seahorse Key with the story of the lowly snake hunter that bested the seasoned pirate. Roughly three miles southwest of Cedar Key, just off of Florida's gulf coast, Seahorse Key gets its name from its shape—an elongated hook jutting into the Gulf of Mexico. The island had always been a bit of a curiosity among sailors. Over 50 feet above sea level, it marks one of the highest points on Florida's western shores.

It is from this elevated vantage point that the rider began to appear, shocking sailors on the waters below. He has always been seen at night atop a golden palomino, a bloodied cutlass at his side. Every sailor who ever saw him would gasp in horror at the sight, for the glowing rider making his rounds along island's rim was also headless.

For years, the headless rider of Seahorse Key was a whispered rumor among seafaring men, a hair-raising tale told around bar tables in every port from New Orleans to Jacksonville. It was only a matter of time before story-tellers connected the headless horseman to the snake hunter's tale of the murder of Pierre LeBlanc and Jean Laffite's stolen booty. And so was born the legend of the headless rider of Seahorse Key.

Today, Seahorse Key is designated a national wildlife refuge, preserved to provide a haven for an endangered group of brown pelicans. The public isn't allowed onto the key, and the only people who visit regularly are marine biologists from the University of Florida, who make the trip to study in a research office situated on the island. To this day, it can only be reached by boat.

Other than the research station and a long-abandoned lighthouse, Seahorse Key is still much like it was over 200 years ago, when Pierre LeBlanc lost his head on the edge of his own cutlass. As for whether or not the cantankerous pirate still makes his rounds of the island, well, that's another question. Though sightings have been reported among the marine biologists that make use of the island's research station, there are enough rumors, enough second- and third-hand accounts that suggest things aren't quite right at Seahorse Key.

According to these rumors, the headless pirate is still there. He's seen by mariners who happen to be on the water after the sun goes down—a faintly glowing apparition sitting atop his horse. Sometimes he's described to be as still as a statue, facing the water with reins in hand; sometimes he's on the move, his spectral horse making its way slowly over the island's high ground. No one who's laid eyes on the ghostly sentry has landed on the key to take a closer look. Or at least no telling of such an adventure exists. Surprising, really, considering no one knows for certain what happened to the rest of Jean Laffite's treasure. The famous pirate probablyreclaimed it on his way out of New Orleans. But there is no way to be sure. Did the snake hunter eventually gather his courage and go back to claim the rest of the booty? Was it swept out to sea? Could someone else have reached it before Laffite?

Impossible to say, though one may wonder if LeBlanc's headless apparition knows the answer to these questions. Or his presence answer enough? Though headless riders are common enough in ghost lore around the world, their stories are never cheerful ones, and more often than not, they are cursed souls, tormented by their earthly ends. Does LeBlanc's disfigured apparition tell us anything about the fate of Laffite's treasure? Perhaps when Jean Laffite finally did make it back to Seahorse Key, LeBlanc's body had washed out to sea, and the treasure was gone. Did Laffite, assuming his shipmate had made away with the booty, utter a curse of such vitriol that Le Blanc felt it beyond the mortal pale? Could this curse have bound him to his eternal patrol of the solitary gulf key? Does LeBlanc remain because the treasure is still there? Or perhaps it's possible that he's still waiting for Jean Lafitte, who for whatever reason was never able to return to Seahorse Key?

As with so many other questions regarding the supernatural, these must go unanswered. Still, with a pirate's treasure and a supernatural legend in the balance, it's likely a matter of time before someone tries to get to the bottom of the old folktale. Anyone who does, however, best hope that the past two centuries have taken the edge off LeBlanc's cutlass and the ire from his disposition.

The Ghosts of the Kingsley Plantation

The idea of plantation culture in the Old South has a way of contradicting itself. On one hand, there is that romanticized idea of Southern belles, gentlemen callers, mint juleps and idyllic landscapes. On the other, there is the brutality of slavery and everything associated with it—the dehumanizing racism, the backbreaking work of picking cotton, the cruel overseers. How do we choose to take in the era? *Gone With The Wind* or *Roots?* Which one defines the way we look at the historic plantations of the Old South?

The truth is that many people entertain both notions at the same time: the Plantation culture before the Civil War can exist as both, a brutal system of oppression and a nostalgic symbol of a bygone age. As far as ghost stories go, nothing sums this up better than the two supernatural accounts that have long circulated around the old Kingsley Plantation in Jacksonville.

Seeing Red in the Rearview Mirror

The realities of slavery, as it once stood in the United States, are so inhumane, so freakishly cruel, that it can be difficult for people today to truly comprehend them. Captured in Africa, shipped across the Atlantic in conditions not suitable for animals and sold off to the highest bidder—women, men and children were torn from homelands, tribes and families to fatten the wallets of southern plantation owners. For the most part, slave-owners justified the institution by telling themselves that blacks were less than human. And the slaves? How did the slaves endure? Some became religious. Some put their backs to the work. Some turned bad.

One of the latter was said to have worked on the Kingsley Plantation. If his name survived the journey from his home to the United States, it hasn't survived the passage of time. Although the man's name has long been forgotten, his actions have not. Indeed, his deeds, vicious and depraved, form the infamous legend that blights the Kingsley Plantation.

If he had potential for such evil on the day he was born, or whether his experiences in the world were to blame, there can be no doubting one fact: the man was evil. Anyone who looked into his eyes knew this. He was pure malice; some said his irises glowed with it—a faint burning red. He would end up painting this maliciousness in blood all over the walls of the one of the slave quarters, where the mutilated bodies of three black women were found. The women had been tortured, raped and murdered, left there for all the others who worked the Kingsley Plantation to see.

Everyone instantly suspected the man with the hate in his eyes, and it didn't take long for severe plantation justice to be meted out. Without a trial or a second guess, he was caught, bound and hanged to death from the branch of an oak tree that grew next to the plantation's main road. And so the Kingsley Plantation's most unpopular slave met his end—a brutal demise tragically appropriate for his brutal life. But if those who lived on Kingsley thought they'd seen the last of this man's burning gaze, they were sorely mistaken.

For it wasn't long afterward that word of a bizarre and unsettling occurrence began to spread through the plantation. The slaves were the ones who noticed it first. "The red eyes," they would whisper in their quarters after the sun went down. "The red eyes have come out again. They're burnin' on the road by the ol' oak tree."

They came out on especially oppressive nights, when torturous heat and humidity seemed to make the very the walls of the slaves' quarters sweat. It was on those sweltering Florida nights, when sleep was near impossible, that the two red orbs were seen glowing by the oak tree where the slave accused of murder had been hanged. Sometimes they were seen from a distance, twin balls of red light hovering in the darkness, filling anyone who saw them with an inexplicable sense of dread. But it was always worse when there was someone out on the road— especially if that someone was a young woman.

Women walking by the oak tree on such nights were often hit with the feeling first. Foreboding fear—a sense that someone, or something, lurked in the darkness among the trees, intent on doing them harm. The feeling was intense enough that those who did not break and run would at least quicken their pace, always just before the red glow emerged from the woods. With the red light came increased panic and the undeniable impression that something was coming after them, and fast.

Always, it turned into a chase with the quarry running as fast as they could from whatever might be behind them. Those who had the courage to look over their shoulders would see this *thing:* nothing more than two red lights, a pair of blazing angry eyes disembodied in the air, coming closer and closer. It might be reasoned that mere eyes with no body can do no harm to anyone, yet such reasoning did nothing for those who got a good look at their pursuer. An unspoken threat seemed to emanate from those malevolent orbs. One look and fear turned to terror.

The red eyes never did overtake any of the slaves it chased, yet word of the phenomenon spread quickly. From the slave quarters to the plantation house to the surrounding countryside, it wasn't long before the tale of "Old Red Eyes," "Watch out for Old Red Eyes," was regularly recounted with a laugh to anyone who was planning on traveling the region at night. Yet, for those who lived and worked at the Kingsley Plantation, Old Red Eyes was no laughing matter, especially for those who found themselves walking alone down the main road at night.

The Kingsley Plantation still stands today, now a historical site located on Fort George Island in the Timucuan Ecological and Historic Preserve, Jacksonville. As for Old

Red Eyes, no one ever actually walks the road into Kingsley in the dark anymore, though people do occasionally drive it. The occasional story from these motorists keeps the legend of Old Red Eyes alive.

Despite the passage of years, Old Red Eyes has made sure that nothing on the road into the Kingsley Plantation has changed. It still prefers especially hot nights, always emerges from the trees behind commuters just after they have passed and prefers terrorizing women over men. Except, now, of course, he pursues women in their automobiles. Not that the enclosed space of a vehicle makes the encounter any less harrowing. Lone motorists have told of being seized by the same sort of intangible terror while driving down the road, where headlights suddenly cast the surrounding bush in an ominous light. Then, just as drivers are thinking how nice it would be to leave the eerie place behind, they appear—two red balls of light, glowing in the rearview mirror.

Even for those who know nothing of the three murdered women or of the slave killed by the roadside, the sight of the two glowing orbs often provokes the same terror that it did among the first witnesses, so many years ago. The first instinct is to hit the gas. Then, when it becomes obvious that the red lights are somehow keeping up and even approaching, the victim's understanding that they are being chased, and that whatever it is isn't friendly, sets in. The closer the lights get in the rearview mirror, the greater the sense of dread. Some have reached potentially perilous speeds trying to out-drive the red orbs. But in the end, Old Red Eyes vanishes on his own, leaving frazzled motorists alone once again, staring into the dark.

The road haunted by Old Red Eyes, leading into the Kingsley Plantation.

So it seems that Old Red Eyes has lost none of his malice over the years. It still remains by the road into Kingsley, all too eager to terrorize women who travel alone, though no one can say with any certainty why. It may simply be that he's an evil ghost, lingering around his site of execution, motivated by nothing other than pure evil. Certainly, this is the popular assumption among paranormal enthusiasts who have studied the matter: a violently misogynistic man who was evil in life continues to be so in death, deriving what pleasure is left him by frightening lone women. The intense fear that women feel at the sight of him comes, perhaps, from a subconscious knowledge of what crimes the spirit would commit if only he was able.

Yet, it is impossible to say for sure. It might very well be that Old Red Eyes is just angry, pure and simple, and that the homicidal tendencies attributed to him just make him angrier. Could it be that the slave who was hanged from the oak tree so many years ago was innocent of the crime he was accused of? Suspected, judged guilty and executed all in the same day, is it possible that his greatest crime was a look that put people on edge? Maybe the entity that remains behind is the tortured spirit of a man who knows he was killed for crimes he didn't commit.

But then, some may counter, if Old Red Eyes was sentenced for a crime he didn't commit, why is it that his ghost choses to harrass lone women on the road at night? Doesn't this constitute a pattern, a hostility toward women, portrayed while he was alive? It may. Unless he was actually innocent, and thus aware, of course, that the real killer, the man who had tortured and murdered the three women on the Kingsley Plantation, was still at large. A stretch, perhaps, but is there a possibility that the ominous feelings Old Red Eyes inspires are a warning rather than a threat? Could it be that the early appearances of Red Eyes to the first women who saw him were intended to get them off the road and to their quarters as quickly as possible? And perhaps the ghost of the former slave has no idea how much time has passed, and maintains his misguided vigil over the road for fear of a danger that has long since passed.

Obviously, this is all speculative, but considering that Old Red Eyes was a man without a voice, who never had the benefit of a formal investigation or a trial, so too is the real story of his legend, and probably forever will be.

An Uncommon Woman of Privilege

The other ghost said to haunt Kingsley is also bound to the plantation long after its time. But the tale of Anna Madgigine Jai isn't nearly so dark as that of the ghost that haunts the road leading onto the property. The legend of Old Red Eyes finds its roots in violence and murder, but the ghost of Anna Jai, a former resident of the Kingsley Plantation, is most likely there because she chooses to be. Considering the way in which her extraordinary life was tied to the plantation house, it's easy to see why.

The year was 1806 and Zephaniah Kingsley, patriarch of the plantation that bore his name, was in Havana, Cuba on business, when he laid eyes on Anna Madgigine Jai for the first time. She was a Senegalese girl who'd been a captive of war in her homeland, sold into slavery and shipped across the Atlantic to the Caribbean markets. This brutal chain of events had led her to the Havana auction block— to a strange land, standing under the oppressive sun and the appraisal of many slave owners. What was it about her that moved Kingsley? History doesn't say, though it was enough to move him to purchase her without hesitation, take her back to his Florida plantation and promptly appoint her his household manager.

She was a skilled supervisor, and the plantation house ran well under her administration. As for Zephaniah, whatever feelings possessed him when he first saw her only grew with time. Before long, Kingsley and Anna were wed. They had four children, and Zephaniah had her officially emancipated in 1811. Within a year, Anna began building her own business, purchasing farmland and slaves of her own.

In many ways, the Kingsley Plantation was like any other in the American South. Driven primarily by slave labor, it was an agrarian enterprise, growing cotton, sugar cane, corn and citrus. And yet, the fact that its matriarch was a former slave also made it quite different from other antebellum plantations. Unlike so many other slaves across the southern states, some of the more skilled collected wages from Zephaniah, while all others were permitted to run their own enterprises after their daily obligations to their master had been completed. Slaves were permitted to keep any profits they made from these operations. It was still slavery of course, but it was slavery with a modicum, just a scrap of humanity, and, compared to what was happening in the neighboring states, it was working reasonably well. The Kingsley slaves were able to tuck away small sums for themselves, while Zephaniah and Anna amassed a fortune. At its peak, the Kingsley empire included four major plantations spanning over 32,000 acres, with roughly 300 slaves.

It wasn't destined to last, however. The first hint of trouble came in 1821, when the United States took over the Florida Territory from Spain. Laws governing race relations under Spanish rule proved to be far more liberal than they were under the United States. Deeming the free blacks in the newly acquired territory a dangerous example to set among the enslaved populations, the Florida legislature went about rectifying the problem, as they saw it. In 1837, laws were passed that made interracial marriages illegal, while severely curtailing the rights of all other blacks, whether free or in bondage. The punishments for any infringements against these laws were harsh.

Zephaniah was unwilling to have his wife and children subjected to these laws, and he began scheming a way out. That way out was Haiti. After purchasing a significant chunk of land on the island, he put his wife in charge of the Kingsley colony, where she looked after their children and governed the workforce of 50 slaves that Zephaniah had freed and sent with his family. After Zephaniah passed away, Anna and her children took over management, running their plantations both in northern Florida and in Haiti. Undaunted by the escalating racial tensions in Florida, Anna returned to the Kingsley Plantation more than once during this period, continuing to buy and sell land and sue whites who were infringing on her property. She went about her business in the territory without fear and became a leader among Florida's free blacks.

She lived to see the abolition of slavery and the defeat of the Confederate army in 1865. An old lady by then, she was able to return to Florida and enjoy what little life she had left as a free citizen of the United States. She was 77 years old in 1870, when she passed away. Given how extraordinary her life was, Anna's passing was hardly acknowledged, and she ended up buried in an unmarked grave, practically forgotten in the records of American history.

Almost, but not quite, for though next to no one noticed when this great woman was laid to rest, the spirit of Anna Madgigine Jai would always be sure to remind anyone staying at the Kingsley Plantation that she once ran the household. There is no specific date for the first sighting of Anna Jai's ghost, but it was certainly some time in the late 1800s, soon after she had passed.

There was talk of a woman's shadowy figure that often appeared on the front porch, always standing before those approaching the house and remaining visible for only a few seconds before vanishing. Inside the house, there were footsteps in the halls. More than one person would claim to hear a woman's voice, clear but distant, with a trace of an echo, as if coming from the other end of a long tunnel. None of the woman's words were intelligible, but everyone who heard them spoke of the voice's definite tone of command.

Did those who experienced these phenomena have Anna Jai's name on their minds? It's tough to say for certain, but author and paranormal enthusiast Joyce Elson Moore surely did when she went to the Kingsley Plantation while researching for her book, *Haunt Hunter's Guide to Florida* (1998). During her investigation, Moore spoke with a woman named Frances Duncan, a tour guide who worked in the plantation house. According to this woman, all sorts of strange things were going on there.

Sometimes these strange things were nothing more than "eerie feelings" that came over her when she was in the house by herself—an indescribable sense that she wasn't alone, even though she knew there was no one else around. Although she never felt threatened by this presence, on some occasions it would manifest itself in far more dramatic ways. She spoke of a ranger who found his way into the kitchen blocked by a chair that was propped against the closed door. This door was the only way in or

It has been reported that the ghost of Anna Madgigine Jai has been seen on the front porch (above) of the Kingsley Plantation.

out of the room; the only way the chair could have been placed on the other side was if it had moved there on its own. Whatever had been in the kitchen obviously didn't want to be disturbed. But what, exactly, was in the kitchen? Neither Duncan nor the ranger tried to think too much about it.

If it was the spirit of Anna Jai, she wasn't so inhospitable to all who ventured into her kitchen. Indeed, there is reason to believe she enjoyed having guests—enough to go out of her way to do a bit of ghostly baking for them. Duncan is quoted as saying: "When I'd lead a tour into the warming kitchen, people would remark, 'Who's cooking gingerbread?' You could smell gingerbread real strong in there. When you got out of the warming kitchen, you couldn't smell it."

Perhaps the comforting smell of gingerbread was her way of welcoming guests to her house. Conversely, drenching people with the supernatural equivalent of ice water might have been her way of expressing displeasure. If this is true, it displeased her greatly when people had the audacity to address her former master by name.

Frances Duncan discovered this one afternoon as she was closing up the house. Just as she'd always done, the tour guide was making her rounds through the house, making sure everything was where it ought to be before shutting down. Finished on the second floor, she began making her way down the stairs, when, on a goofy impulse, she called out "Goodnight, Mr. Kingsley!" into the empty house. What followed nearly made her jump out of her skin. A near-paralyzing cold hit her, which Duncan likened to a bucket of cold water being dumped over her. Shivering violently and covered in goose bumps, Frances wasted no time getting out of the house. She went directly to a ranger that afternoon, telling him what she had experienced on the stairs. A month later, the ranger approached Frances, telling her that curiosity had gotten the better of him, and that he too tried bidding Zephaniah a good night right around closing time.

"What happened?" Frances asked.

"Somebody poured ice water on me," was his reply.

Frances made a point from then on to avoid saying anything out loud about Zephaniah Kinglsey, but on one other occasion, she did work up the courage to confront Anna directly. The problem centered on a bed in one of the upstairs rooms. According to Frances, this bed's rightful place was about two feet from one of the walls, with its end against a window. That was where it *belonged*. But every time she opened up in the morning, she noticed that the bed had been moved, pulled about 15 inches from the window. While pushing the bed back, she noticed that there were grooves worn into the floor from a constant push and pull over the years. Apparently, she wasn't the only employee who'd had this problem.

This continued for a while, until the frustrated tour guide went to the park supervisor for suggestions. He came up, took a look at the grooves in the floor, looked at Frances, and asked: "Well, what do you think it is?"

"I don't know," Frances replied, "but every morning when I come in here that bed is pulled out, and there are grooves in this floor where this has been going on for quite a while."

"Well," he offered, "it looks like it." And that was the extent of his advice.

Frances knew she'd have to deal with the situation on her own. The breaking point came one morning when, while looking at the bed that had been moved once again, Frances decided she'd had enough of this little game. "Okay!" Frances hollered into the empty room. "You want the bed in the middle of the floor, *leave* the bed in the middle of the floor." She turned around and stormed out of the room.

Considering that Frances didn't move the bed back that day and never tried to again, it might be said that Anna was the one who ended up winning the little battle of wills over where the bed belonged. Neither the bed nor anything else in the room was ever moved again. Could the ghost of Anna Jai have decided that she'd tested the tour guide enough, and decided to leave well enough alone in the upstairs room after that? Maybe, maybe not, though this is what Frances Duncan would probably like to believe.

In her investigation of the Kingsley House, Joyce Elison Moore claimed to capture a photograph of what she believes to be the ghost of Anna Jai standing on the porch. If so, this would be the first time anyone has ever captured an image of the spirit said to haunt the plantation house. After years of remaining invisible to human eyes, has Anna Jai decided to emerge before people? Why now, after all these years? Like so much else about this fascinating historical figure, we will likely never know.

2
Haunted Houses

Ma Barker and her Boy

Who was Ma Barker? It depends who you ask. Anyone getting their information from the American government—in this case, J. Edgar Hoover's Justice Department in the 1930s—would walk away with a picture of a ruthless criminal mastermind heading a homicidal gang of thugs with no qualms about killing people to further her nefarious ends. Hoover himself called her "a veritable beast of prey."

Yet, if you were to ask some of the people who knew her, you'd learn of an entirely different person. These are the words of Alvin Karpis, one of the ringleaders of the Barker-Karpis gang:

> Ma was always somebody in our lives. Love didn't enter into it really. She was somebody we looked after and took with us when we moved from city to city, hideout to hideout…It's no insult to Ma's memory that she just didn't have the brains or the know-how to direct us on a robbery. It wouldn't have occurred to her to get involved in our business, and we always made a point of only discussing our scores when Ma wasn't around. We'd leave her at home when we were arranging a job, or we'd send her to a movie. Ma saw a lot of movies.

This version shows Ma Barker as an innocent old lady, a simple hillbilly whose only crime was her fervent loyalty to her four boys, Herman, Lloyd, Arthur and Frederick, whom she believed to be the sweetest sons any mother could have, no matter how many brutal crimes they committed. Whatever version the reader subscribes to, whether Ma was the vicious matriarch of the Barker-Karpis gang, or an unwitting innocent dragged from one hideout to another, there can be no denying her ultimate end. Guilty or innocent of the charges laid against her by the United States Justice Department, she died an outlaw—holed up in a hideout, staring down a group of Federal agents.

Before she was Ma Barker, she was Arizona Clark, a Springfield, Missouri native who was born in the hardscrabble America of the late 19th century. When she was 14, she married an Ozark miner named George Barker. George would never participate in the crime spree that would make his last name famous in the annals of American criminal history, but each of his four sons showed potential for brutality early on in life. By the time they were teenagers, the Barker boys were getting into all sorts of trouble. Their withdrawn father seemed to have no opinion whenever neighbors came by to complain about his sons, and Ma Barker had no shortage of curses to hurl at anyone who suggested that her boys might be anything short of perfect.

The Barker boys wouldn't forget their mother's devotion, and they decided to take her with them in 1931, when they began their four-year crime spree. American history shows that outlaws on the lam never last too long, and the Barker boys were no exception. They dropped off one by one, killed or caught and dragged to

Ma Barker

jail throughout the early '30s, until all that was left was
Ma and her youngest, Fred.

Believing the vast swampland of Florida would provide
as good a hideout as any, the pair found a secluded house
overlooking Lake Weir, near the town of Ocklawaha, in
Marion County. Ma and Fred did very little to draw attention to themselves in the short time they called Florida
home. But still, Hoover's fledgling FBI was relentless, and
they eventually closed in on the pair.

It was early in the morning of January 16, 1935, when
agents crept up to the two-story home. The small army of

officers positioned themselves around the house and agent E.J. Connelly walked up to the front porch and knocked on the door. Ma Barker answered, the 63-year-old woman squinting suspiciously at the armed man standing at her door.

Special Agent Connelly introduced himself. "Ma Barker," he said, "the FBI is here to arrest your son, Fred Barker. We know he's inside."

Looking past Connelly, Ma Barker squinted harder at the yard. Her look went back to the agent on the porch. The elderly woman looked a bit confused when she nodded, mumbled something and went in to fetch her son, or so Connelly may have assumed. But if he had made such an assumption, he would have assumed wrong.

When Fred Barker appeared at the doorway, it was with a grin and a loaded Tommy gun. Somehow, Connelly managed to get away unscathed, turning and bolting as Fred lowered his machine gun and sprayed the porch with lead. The agents stationed around the house responded instantly, and the exchange that followed would go down as the longest gunfight in the FBI's history.

In over four hours of continuous fire, the Federal agents emptied about 1500 rounds into the house, ripping it to pieces with machine gun slugs and buckshot, not stopping until all return fire from the house had ceased completely, until they were sure that no one inside could have possibly survived. And even then, they weren't confident. They sent in Willie Woodberry, the Barkers' gardener, to make sure that the inhabitants were really dead.

"It's me, Ma! Don't shoot!" the justifiably frightened gardener shouted as he walked through the shattered and

smoking doorway and into the devastated house. Everything inside was riddled with holes. "Ma?" Willie called
again. There was no response.

It turned out that the Federal agents had accomplished
what they'd set out to do. Nothing had survived the four-
hour barrage they'd laid on the house. They found Ma
with her son, Fred, on the top floor, a machine gun lying
on the ground between them. Both dead. Although Fred
was perforated by countless bullet holes, Ma had only
been hit once—but once had been enough. The Barker
clan had finally been stopped, with every criminal in the
family either dead or behind bars.

Yet history tells us that the figurehead of the infamous
family hadn't been so vilified until *after* she was killed.
Indeed, only then did the head of the Justice Department
begin talking about the old woman as though she'd been a
threat to national security. The cynics have reasoned that
J. Edgar Hoover slandered the old woman's name to jus-
tify her death at the hands of his agents. In this case, the
cynics are more than likely right. Not only has there never
been any solid evidence that suggests Ma Barker was
involved with any of her sons' crimes, but the incredulous
responses of men such as Alvin Karpis makes the truth
uncomfortably clear. Ma Barker, the "veritable beast of
prey," was a Justice Department fabrication, invented to
explain the murder of a 63-year-old woman who was only
guilty of excessive devotion to her sons.

Like in every other account in this book, however,
death hardly marks the end of the tale, and as readers
might suspect, this isn't all there is to Ma Barker's story.
The strange goings on at the Lake Weir home began soon

after Ma and Fred were buried. The ones most curious to get a look at the place where Ma Barker met her end were the first to talk about the sounds.

They were usually heard in the early morning or late at night by those creeping up to the bullet-ridden house. Sometimes there were the sounds of a card game filtering out through the shattered parlor window—the fluttering of a deck of cards being shuffled, chairs creaking, bets being thrown down on a wooden table. Other times, people swore they heard slow, measured footsteps making their way down a hall and up the creaking staircase.

The bravery of those investigating the house seemed to increase by increments. Many who heard the eerie sounds coming from the shot-out husk of a home decided to stop their snooping, but others found themselves drawn to the now-ominous Marion County home. More stories began to circulate around Marion County. There was talk of a moving figure spotted through the bullet holes. One particularly brave investigator, said to have ventured inside, claimed to see an old woman with dark hair climbing the stairs as he entered. The moment he crossed the threshold, the woman turned to look at him, and the sight of her blank gaze sent him running and filled with terror.

It wasn't long before accounts of people venturing upstairs began to get around. According to these stories, the phenomena occurring on the second floor were far more dramatic than what was going on downstairs. In the room where Ma and Fred's bodies were found, shouting voices were heard on more than one occasion. The voices were said to be muffled, as though coming from a great distance, so it was impossible to make out exactly what was being said. But it was obvious to anyone who listened closely that there were two voices: one belonging to a man, the other, to a woman.

People concluded, of course, that the man was Fred Barker, and the woman—who else? If Ma Barker was truly shouting at her son from the room where she was shot, was she also the one seen engaged in a far more peaceful activity by a number of people in another second floor room, standing with her face to the wall, combing her dark hair? No one who has seen this apparition has stood around long enough to see what happens next, and there are no accounts of anyone trying to ask Ma any questions. As a matter of fact, the first instinct that has seized those who have stumbled upon the woman with the dark hair is to turn around and head the other way without delay. No one, it seems, has been too eager to see Ma Barker turn around.

The house where Ma and Fred were gunned down is still standing today, though there are far fewer accounts of weird goings-on. Privately owned and fronted by high hedges, the house isn't easy to see from the road, and the owners are understandably hesitant at opening their doors to every paranormal enthusiast in Florida, so it is impossible to say what has become of the two ghosts. Are they still haunting the house where they were killed, continuing some spectral card game that neither can hope to win, arguing about something on the second floor? Is Ma Barker still seen facing the wall, pulling a comb through her hair? Let's hope not, for the sake of the people living there today.

Winter Home in Sarasota

"I'd never been there before, but my parents had nothing but good things to say about their place in Sarasota. It was their dream to have a winter home in Florida, and it took them until they were retired to be living it, but hey, late's better than never, eh?" says "Sarah Tooley," a woman who requests anonymity out of respect for her parents' privacy and her own skittishness. "I don't know what my folks would say if I they found out I was telling people that all sorts of weird stuff was going on in their dream home, but I don't imagine they'd be too thrilled about it."

Nevertheless, despite being shy about attaching her name to her experiences in Sarasota, the energy in her voice suggests that Sarah has a real eagerness to tell her story. "I've read a lot of ghost stories," Sarah begins, "and one of the things that stands out for me is how easy some supposed ghosts would be to ignore if you ever ran into them, you know? For instance, one of the common ones you hear about is cold spots. Often you hear, 'I was walking down the hall and suddenly I felt this cold spot,' or else, 'All of a sudden I felt my hair on the back of my neck stand up, and instantly, I knew there was a ghost around.'

"Honestly, if I ever ran into a cold spot walking down a hall, I think I'd just keep on walking. Cold spot—so what? I get chills all the time and I don't even think about it. As for the hairs on the back of the neck, seems to me they are just waiting for an excuse to stand up and give me the tingles. Really, they shoot up in half the movies I see, along with the ones on my arms."

Unimpressed as she may have been by cold spots and goose bumps, Sarah's own supernatural experiences in her parents' home turned out to be far more dramatic. "The things I went through when I was there by myself were pretty crazy," she says. "Believe me when I say that cold spots and chills were the least of my problems."

The trouble began on her first night there. "I'd never been to Florida before, and that year, I needed a bit of a break from a winter that just didn't want to end," Sarah says. "My parents usually stay from November to early March. They had just returned from spending the winter, and the place was empty. I was looking forward to having some time alone in the sun."

The lure of time in the sun is exactly what attracts most of Sarasota's winter residents; retired snowbirds like Sarah's parents arrive in yearly droves. Known for its beaches, golf courses, quality dining and fine boating, the sunny city on the Gulf is not the sort of place one might imagine ghosts to haunt. Spirits of the dead were definitely the last thing on Sarah's mind: "I think the fewer details I give about the location of the house, the better, but I will say that I was really impressed. My parents had found a place in a beautiful neighborhood where houses were well looked after and all quite new. It was early afternoon when I arrived, and the sun lit up the spacious foyer. Like I said before, I've read a lot of ghost stories, and there was nothing about this place that said, 'Get out, dead people live here.'" She would soon discover, however, that not all dead people are unwelcoming.

"First thing I did after unpacking was go for a swim in the Gulf," Sarah says. "I felt relaxed heading back to the

Sarasota

house. The sun was starting to go down and I was looking forward to taking it easy with a book, or maybe watching some TV." But she knew something had changed the moment she stepped through the front door.

"A lump settled in my throat as soon as I shut the door behind me. The house was darker now, and it felt totally changed. There were shadows in the corners, down the hall and into the kitchen. It sounds weird, but the shadows, the way everything looked from the front door gave me the creeps; it was like there was something inside the house. It sounds crazy, but I felt like someone was in the shadows, watching."

Telling herself that the feeling was irrational, Sarah slipped her shoes off and walked to the kitchen. "I did what I think most people would have done," Sarah says. "I told myself it was all in my head and just tried to ignore it. Well, that didn't work."

She saw it just before she stepped into the room. "I was walking fast to the kitchen, trying to keep from looking down the hall leading to the bedrooms, which was really dark. I couldn't shake this feeling that there was something in the shadows there. Not anyone specific, not anyone I could see, but the shadow in the hall just felt like it was alive. The feeling grew as I got closer to the kitchen. I remember trying to look away, but I just couldn't. Although my eyes saw nothing there, my gut was telling me something else. I got to the kitchen and flipped on the light, and finally decided to just get away from that hall. I turned to go into the kitchen, and that's when I saw it. The second I turned my head, the shadow moved. I saw it out of the corner of my eye—a big shadow, the shape of a man, moved out of the hall so fast I screamed."

Sarah says she didn't think so much as react, turning to face the black silhouette while backing into the kitchen. "The thing is, as soon as I turned to look at it, it started to disappear. I couldn't have had a clear look at it for more than a few seconds. It never stopped moving. It kept coming forward, but it kind of faded as it came. Next thing I knew, I was standing there in the kitchen, looking at nothing but the empty hall."

In mere seconds, Sarah saw her hopes for a relaxing holiday vanish. "That was it," she says, "After that, the beach and the water and the sun didn't mean a thing. That shadow in the house consumed everything. There was no doubt in my mind. I saw what I saw, and I knew I'd seen a ghost." Although she was in the house with a ghost, her feelings on the matter were surprisingly conflicted.

"It's a tough one to pin down," she says. "So much ended up happening while I was there, but at first, I think I was just as much excited as I was scared." Being an avid reader of ghost stories, Sarah found some part of herself thrilled at the idea of sharing her living space with a ghost. It wouldn't take long for this enthusiasm to fade.

"The next two nights, I kept my eyes peeled," Sarah continues. "Spooky as it was, I wanted to see that shadow again. I was curious. The first time, I'd been too scared to notice any details. This time around, I wanted to get a closer look. Maybe even ask it a few questions or something. It was all I could think about. All day, I was just biting my nails, waiting for the evening. I tried shopping around in town to get my mind off it—no way. Going to the beach didn't work either. For the first two days, I was obsessed with it."

She'd become so preoccupied with seeing the moving shadow again that every shadow in the house started to seem suspicious. She spent hours every evening fixated on the hallway. One night she positioned herself exactly where she'd seen the shadow the first time, and she stood there for most of the evening, adjusting the angle at which she was standing, replaying her entrance and approach to the hallway, thinking that this might trigger the manifestation once again. Nothing.

"Looking back, there's no way I can say for sure whether or not anything out of the ordinary was going on for those first two nights," Sarah says. "I was so buzzed about seeing this ghost that every creak in the house was making me jump. At one point, I mistook two cats meowing outside for something supernatural. I was going a little bit nuts."

On the third night it dawned on her, that she should try a new approach and come at the ghost from another angle. But it still didn't show. And then Sarah began to doubt herself.

"After that third night, I started to wonder if maybe I *had* been seeing things," she says. "It's amazing what two short days can do to your convictions. As sure as I was about what I'd seen, after nothing happened that second night, I started to wonder. I started making excuses: maybe I'd spent too much time in the sun that first day. Or it could have had something to do with the travel—some weird jet lag or something. I don' t know." Yet, her doubts regarding what she'd seen wouldn't last.

"On the fourth night I wasn't feeling the same kind of anxiety as on the previous two," she says. "I'd arrived back from another day at the beach. I was dead tired from all the swimming and sun, and was just thinking about making a bite to eat and going to bed early. That day, when I walked in the door, I'm pretty sure the shadow was the last thing on my mind."

She'd barely taken her sandals off when the air changed. "I just took a step inside and I heard it—a voice, a whispering voice. It said, 'Hello.'" She stopped in her tracks, suddenly wide awake, the cold chill up her back replacing the sun's warm afterglow. "It was a man's voice," Sarah remembers, "and it sounded sort of rushed, stressed out, but not unfriendly."

Not unfriendly but, according to Sarah, very, very creepy. "I stopped the second I heard it, and I could feel my heart hammering away. I was sitting there waiting for it to say something else. It was so quiet and I was trying hard not to even breathe. I didn't want to make a sound out of fear that I might miss it if it spoke again. I stood there for I don't know how long, just waiting. But nothing was happening. I started to wonder if maybe I'd imagined the voice."

Just like she did with the shadow, she began to doubt her senses. Sarah describes the sound as the strangest thing she'd ever heard. It seemed impossible to say where in the house the voice had come from. "It sounded as though it was coming from all around and nowhere at the same time."

As she stood there, as still and silent as she was able, replaying the voice in her head, it dawned on her that she'd been so concerned about analyzing the voice that she'd completely disregarded one simple fact. It had said hello, a greeting, and she'd responded by giving her best deer-in-headlights impression. Maybe she should answer?

"Hello?" Sarah ventured into the house.

"As soon as the words came out of my mouth, I saw something move in the hall, the same hallway where the shadow had emerged the last time," Sarah recalls. "Over the last two days, I'd thought of some questions I wanted to ask: who was he? why was he there? what was it like to be dead and haunting a retired couple's Florida home?" When the time came for Sarah to ask these questions, however, she froze, unable to get a single sound past the colossal lump in her throat. "I guess it was all fine and good in theory," she laughs. "Funny how quickly plans can fall apart."

And so, Sarah just stood there watching the black shape shifting at the end of the darkened hall. "I couldn't see exactly what it was doing. All I can say for sure is that it was moving around—the shadows in the corner were moving. From where I was standing it looked like it was moving really slowly, side-to-side, back and forth. It wasn't like last time, though. It wasn't coming any closer to me." Sarah stood watching the nebulous shadow for several more minutes as it moved in the hall. It remained there the whole time, neither approaching nor fading away.

"It took me a while, but I finally worked up the courage to speak again," Sarah says. "At first, all I could get out was another "hello," but then I pulled myself together and asked who it was, and what it was doing in my parents' house." If Sarah expected a straight answer out of the figure in the hall, she was mistaken. "The second I asked that last question, I knew that I touched a sore spot," she says. "Don't ask me how, I just knew that something weird was going to happen. This crazy chill went right up my back and I had to catch my breath." An instant later, there came a response to Sarah's questions.

"Every one of my parents' wine glasses, which they had hanging from a rack over the sink, went flying off by themselves and smashed onto the floor. Eight wine glasses, just like that. Bang! It happened so fast I wouldn't have believed it if it wasn't for the fact that there was broken glass all over the kitchen floor."

Sarah took a few moments to allow what had just occurred to sink in. Then, when the icy grip of fear relaxed its grip on her spinal column, she turned and walked out of the house. "I went for a long walk. I don't know what, if anything, I was thinking," Sarah says. "I think I needed time to really get a grip on what was going on. This wasn't just a moving shadow anymore. It was wine glasses, real physical objects, being thrown around. Everything seemed so much more real now. There was no more second-guessing what I did or didn't see. My parents had a ghost in their house and I needed to ask myself what I was going to do about it."

The first thing she did was steel herself to go back to the house. Reigning in her fear, she stepped inside. "Right away, it felt different. The creepiness was gone. I didn't believe the ghost was gone for good, but maybe after the incident with the wine glasses, he just needed some time off," Sarah laughs. "Maybe, just like me, he'd taken some time to walk off whatever was bothering him." Sarah was surprised to find that before he'd left, he did a bit of house cleaning. Not only was the broken glass now swept up into one neat corner in the kitchen, but the dishes from that morning were all done and neatly stacked.

"It was one thing that he swept up the wine glasses," Sarah says, "but the fact that he did the dishes just floored me. That was when I started to think that maybe I was totally misunderstanding whatever was living there."

After all, the spirit did greet her with a "hello" when she walked in earlier that night, and now, it had just done some cleaning in the kitchen. Although she had felt paralyzing fear in its presence, there were also times when she'd felt curiously devoid of any apprehension. What was it with these mixed signals? Why did the spirit in the house sometimes feel threatening and sometimes benign? It would be a few days yet before she was able to come up with any answer.

"After the incident in the kitchen, things got way crazier," Sarah explains," and I mean *way* crazier. At first, I had no clue what to make of all of it. This spirit displayed a real Dr. Jekyll and Mr. Hyde character. One second, it would do something completely destructive, like smash a light bulb in its socket or bend all the cutlery I'd put on the table for dinner, then it would turn and do something helpful. On one occasion, I was doing laundry and came into the room and found all my clothes folded and stacked. Almost all the time, unless I got there first, it would clean up whatever mess it had made earlier. Broken light bulbs were never left lying on the floor. With the bent fork and knife, I turned my back for one second to get a new set; by the time I looked again they'd both been bent back."

This pattern of random destruction and restoration repeated itself throughout the rest of the Sarah's stay. "I actually got used to it pretty quickly," she says. "I still got chills when the angry side of the spirit would show itself, but it was usually followed by a calm whenever the pleasant side would make amends." Still, getting used to it didn't mean accepting it as much as it meant resigning herself to it— it didn't take long for the fear and novelty of the supernatural phenomena to be replaced with irritation.

"After the first week, its presence got pretty old," Sarah says. "Thrilling as it was for me at first, after you see a roll of toilet paper unravel itself for the umpteenth time, it gets more annoying than fascinating. I got so used to the shadow in the hallway that twice I just walked straight through it. Once, when it was trying to give me the chills, when I felt that coldness creeping up my back, I just told it to buzz off, and the cold went away, just like that."

The end of the second week couldn't come fast enough, and when it did, Sarah left the house without any intention of coming back. "What can I say? I guess living in a haunted place just isn't for me. I wasn't scared by it, just put off, I guess. I found that I hated living in a place where it always felt like something was *wrong*. Maybe you could compare it to living in a house where all the taps are leaky and there's nothing you can do to fix it. I guess it might have something to do with the fact that I like to be in control, that I like everything to be in its right place, but the randomness of the ghost's activities really started to *annoy* me."

That said, after living in the house for two weeks, Sarah did have a theory about what was going on there. "I still don't know *why* it was happening. The house was fairly new, and I took to asking around the neighborhood about the place—who had lived there previously, if it had any kind of history. No one could tell me anything."

"But I had a thought in the kitchen one day," Sarah continues, "right after an open jar of strawberry jam threw itself off the counter and spilled all over the linoleum. By this time, I knew the drill and left the kitchen to kill a few minutes in the living room; when I got back, the jam was cleaned up off the floor and the jar was back on the counter."

It was then that the realization hit her. "I wasn't dealing with one ghost in this house. There were two. As soon as it occurred to me, I knew it was true. There was no way one entity could be responsible for all this. It just didn't make any sense. Why would anything, even the spirit of a dead person, keep making messes just to clean them up seconds later? Why was it that sometimes, out of the blue, I'd come home to find the living room tidied, or the bed made, or the bathroom cleaned? There was no way the same entity that did this was also smashing glasses and breaking light bulbs."

Two ghosts—one destructive, the other helpful; given the nature of the phenomena, it was a sound enough conclusion. But as for the question of who these spirits were, or why they were haunting the Sarasota home, Sarah has no clue. "I did a bit of research into the matter while I was there. Took a look at the city records, read one local history, asked around, but I couldn't find anything, not one single clue, that offered any kind of explanation. The whole thing was still a total mystery to me by the time I left." A mystery that was only deepened by the fact that her parents had never mentioned anything to their daughter about what was going on in their second home.

"I still don't know what to say about that," she says. "I didn't want to worry them, you know. So I didn't freak out over the whole thing when I talked to them about it." Sarah tried to be subtle when her parents asked her how she enjoyed her stay. "I just asked them if they'd noticed anything strange," she says. "Mom was instantly worried, and I could tell by her voice that they hadn't seen the things that I had seen. The way she said, 'What kind of things?' I could tell the question really took her by surprise." Sarah decided it would be best if she played down the issue, shrugging off questions. "I told her that I'd heard some noises in the backyard a few nights, and thought they might have some kind of animal back there. She told me she'd get Dad to take a look next time they were down."

Sarah still isn't sure what to say about her experiences in Sarasota, and she is even more perplexed that her parents haven't had to deal with the strange shadow. "They still go down there for four months a year," she begins. "So it is one of two things: either they aren't seeing the same things I did, or they are and they're not talking about it. Besides what I've read in books, I don't have any real insight about this stuff. I have never seen ghosts before. I don't think that I'm sensitive to spirits in any way, but I can't explain why my parents have not experienced the same things." Sarah hesitates before continuing. "Maybe it was something with *me* that brought it about. Maybe there is something in that house that reacted to me personally, and is fine with my parents? I don't know. What I do know, though, is that I don't plan on spending too much time there. Not that I have anything against Sarasota—it's a really beautiful place. But hang out in that house again? Spend more time with the ghosts? No thanks. Those two weeks were enough ghosts for a lifetime."

A Violent Haunting
in Deltona

Like so many other paranormal enthusiasts, Dusty Smith is fascinated by history. Founder of the Daytona Beach Paranormal Research Group (DBPRG), she lists her pre-occupation with the past as one of the reasons she is involved in paranormal investigation. In many ways, this ghost hunter also considers herself an amateur historian, sifting through local folklore and historical records and searching for the roots of certain haunted sites. But Dusty is quick to point out that being a history enthusiast living in Dayton Beach can be challenging.

"Daytona isn't conscientious about its history," Dusty says. "In many parts of the world, people have pride in preserving their history, but here, we're amazed when a building survives more than 35 years." Dusty laments that the only historical landmarks of her home state are fighting a losing battle against concrete and steel development.

Despite Daytona's oldest buildings being reduced to rubble under an inexorable advance of bulldozers, there seem to be enough ghosts to keep Dusty busy. Not that she's complaining. "You know, I find the scientific end of paranormal investigation really fascinating. The questions that build when you're out in the field never end. Nobody has come up with any answers yet, and people have been studying this stuff forever." And yet for years now, since Dusty set up the DBPRG in 1997, people have been coming to her with questions about Daytona's history and its hauntings—not such a surprise when one considers what Dusty's been doing for the last few years.

In addition to heading the DBRPG, Dusty also guides groups on her "Haunts of the World's Most Famous Beach" tour, walking guests through some of the town's cemeteries and haunted sites. Although ghosts are certainly a focus of her tour, she also uses the opportunity to educate the sightseers about the history of the town.

"The ghost tour started because of our research group," Dusty says. "Soon after we started investigating, we realized that we needed funds for all of our ghost-hunting equipment." Still, once the DBPRG could afford all the necessary equipment, Dusty felt it wrong to be making money off tours and stories of the town's deceased. "Here I was standing outside this cemetery, talking about and benefiting from these people who are no longer with us. I just couldn't take a paycheck from it." The ghost tour evolved into The International Association of Cemetery Preservationists, Inc.—a group dedicated to the improvement and maintenance of Daytona's graveyards. The association has adopted three cemeteries, which despite the ravages of the occasional hurricane, are in far better shape now than they were under county care.

Founder of the DBPRG, principle guide for the "Haunts of the World's Most Famous Beach" tour and head of the Association of Cemetery Preservationists, Dusty might be called Daytona's resident specialist on paranormal matters. Nevertheless, as is often the case where supernatural phenomena are concerned, even the specialists are sometimes left clueless. That was certainly the case in the investigation of the house in Deltona, about 20 minutes west of Daytona.

Of all the haunted sites the DBPRG has investigated, the nondescript concrete block home stands out in Dusty's mind, so much so that she has just completed a book about her own experiences there. "A young couple contacted me by e-mail in September 2001," Dusty begins. "To tell you the truth, at first I wasn't sure what to make of it—it was full of all sorts of things that seemed a bit over-the-top. I couldn't help wondering if these people were for real, but I thought I'd check it out—do the interview and see what would happen."

It was obvious from the very start of the investigation that the tenants of the Deltona home were dealing with something that the DBPRG had never seen before. Further-more, Dusty's group and the current tenants weren't the only ones who knew there were strong forces at work in the house. During her preliminary tour of the house, Dusty discovered a garage full of unpacked furniture. She was told that it wasn't theirs but belonged to the owner, who moved out of the place in the middle of the night in the spring of 2000, only three weeks after he purchased it. Whatever he experienced in the house must have left an impression because he still gave the front door a wide berth, staying in his car and leaning on his horn when he came to collect the rent.

It didn't take long for the ghosts to manifest them-selves to Dusty and her team. "Right off, we recorded hot spots, cold spots, picked up knocking sounds in the walls. This place had a real nasty haunting going on." It would only get worse.

"Basically," Dusty continues, "what had started as a Friday night party conversation piece, in eight months had turned into a very dangerous situation." Yet as the phenomena in the house grew evermore dramatic, Dusty's determination to study it also increased. At the beginning, she was spending an average of two nights a week in Deltona; by the end of the case, she was there almost every night.

"It was incredible," Dusty recalls. "In that first week, we were getting activity from three of four spots at the same time. To me that denotes there is more than one 'entity' on site. There would be a hot spot or a cold spot in the baby's room, banging noises in the hallway and a mist forming on the back roof of the house all at the same time."

"On top of it," Dusty continues, "our EVP readings were crazy." EVP, or Electronic Voice Phenomena, is one way investigators determine the presence of ghosts. It is a common theory among ghost hunters that spirits often emit sounds imperceptible to the human ear, but which can be heard when played back on audio recording devices.

"When we listened to our recorders after our investigations, there were so many voices, it sounded like a cocktail party going on." If so, no one at this ghostly soiree seemed to be having much fun. The voices sounded harried, frantic, dispersed with growling noises and something that sounded like someone vomiting violently. Every now and then, they could make out barely legible speech. Whoever or whatever was speaking wasn't too happy that the ghost hunters were there: "What are you doing here?" they heard the voice say over and over again.

With each passing week, as the phenomena grew more and more intense, so too did the DBPRG's hope of reaching any conclusions. Dusty recalls how lost she felt in her search for an explanation. "Three months into it, I was absolutely stumped. I checked all of the background history, all the building records and property records and anything I could get my hands on." Nothing. This was a standard Florida concrete block home, built in 1968, with no outstanding events in its history. She found only one death associated with the property—an elderly woman who died peacefully a few years before. Dusty and the DBPRG could not see how a solitary old woman dying of natural causes could be responsible for the carnage they were witnessing.

And then things got worse. In December, right around Christmas, Dusty was attacked. She recalls: "The tenant and I were standing next to a set of golf clubs, talking about something, when his wife came by and told him to lay the clubs down, just to keep their baby from knocking them over and hurting herself. While I was standing there watching him lower the bag, it suddenly lifted off the floor and slammed me right in the midsection."

The DBPRG contacted other members in the ghost hunting community for advice, including established investigators such as Troy Taylor in Illinois and Dave Juliano in New Jersey. Juliano and Taylor promptly got back to Dusty, but even these ghost-hunting luminaries were stumped, suggesting that she either consult a psychic or leave the house altogether before other people got hurt.

Taking their advice, Dusty sent photos to Kelly Weaver, a well-known psychic residing in Pennsylvania, and then went to the tenants. With three broken ribs rattling in her chest, she decided to level with them. "I told them the DBPRG could keep coming back to the house, documenting this phenomena, getting really great pictures, EVPs and video footage, but that it was time for them to make a decision. They were renting. They could move out at any time. And the situation was getting more dangerous."

If, at first, the family hesitated at taking these words to heart, the events of early January 2002 convinced them it was time to pack their bags. By that time, the DBPRG had isolated the most extreme activity just outside the baby's room, and they set up night vision surveillance cameras inside, monitoring the cradle. The footage from this camera ultimately ended both the family's stay in the house and the DBPRG's investigation of the site.

To this day, Dusty shudders when she recalls the tape. "The footage opens with the mother putting her baby into the crib; she turns on the little music box attached to the side of the crib, gives the baby her bottle and then turns off the light. It is only a few minutes after her mother leaves and you can still hear the baby. She is barely sucking on the bottle, so you know she is almost asleep. You can still hear the music box playing—everything's fine. And then out of nowhere, you hear this voice."

It came out clearly on the audio: "Oh, Emmy."

But it wasn't spoken affectionately. Dusty describes the voice as neither male nor female, but something about the tone gave the DBPRG founder goosebumps when she heard it. "We stopped the tape there and played it back several times to make sure we were not imagining it. The baby must have heard it too because she sat up in her crib.

What followed was a truly bizarre exchange. The 18-month-old child was spouting garbled baby talk into the darkness, and was answered with a guttural stream of growls that left Dusty's blood cold. "All of a sudden, on the tape, we could see a gray, transparent blob of mist come from the center of the room, up over the crib rail and into the crib."

That was when the child's nonchalant baby talk turned into something else. "The baby started screaming—loud. We could hear her screaming 'No! No! No!' over and over again. On the tape, this went on for 45 minutes. She was screaming at the top of her voice for 45 minutes."

Not wasting any time, Dusty picked up the telephone and called the house. "I told them to get the baby out of her room, and then I headed over there as fast as I could."

By the time Dusty arrived, the parents were in their bedroom, putting their daughter's crib back together after relocating it. "Of course, the first thing they asked me was what was on the tape. I didn't want to upset them," Dusty says, "but I needed to get across that they were in danger and really should leave the house."

Dusty's attempts at tact were rendered meaningless, however, when the girl came toddling into the room. "The moment I turned around to look at her, the crib rail came off the floor, over the corner of the bed and pinned her to the floor. It took all three of us to get that crib rail off that kid."

"Needless to say, the family didn't stick around too much longer after that. The mother and daughter left for Maryland to stay with her parents, while the father stayed behind to close up the house and find a new place to live.

He stayed for about three weeks, spending most of his nights at the neighbor's house," Dusty recalls.

During this period, the DBPRG heard back from Kelly Weaver about the photos Dusty had sent. Apparently, the house's bad energy was able to reach as far as Pennsylvania, where Ms. Weaver found herself having a difficult time with the package from Florida. "She told us that it took her quite a while to even open the envelope because she'd feel physically ill whenever she would touch it," Dusty says. When she felt able to study the photographs, the Pennsylvania psychic got back to Dusty immediately. "Basically, most of what she told us we already knew," the DBPRG founder says. "The activity in the house was centered around the baby's room." Interestingly, Dusty did learn that the doorway to the room was mysteriously located right under the peak of the house. Why is that interesting?

The forces that possessed the Deltona house were not happy about the baby's location. A few days after the mother and baby left, Dusty received a bone-chilling e-mail sent out from the family's address to her ghost tours address. It contained two simple questions. Although the words were riddled with strange punctuation and horribly misspelled, Dusty could make out the questions. They asked: "Where is the baby? How is the baby?"

Dusty headed to the house posthaste, making a beeline for the family's computer when she got there. Checking the log of sent e-mails on their server, she found no such message directed to her address. Furthermore, the DBPRG e-mail had been added to the address list, which automatically occurs when an e-mail is sent out from a site, but the tour's address was not saved anywhere on this list. Dusty believed the husband when he told her he hadn't sent out the message.

The fact that whatever was haunting the house was also computer savvy did nothing to ease Dusty's preoccupation with the Deltona case. "I have to say, this case really got to me," she says. "Not only were the findings so off the charts compared to anything we'd done before, but as much time as I put into it, I couldn't find *any* explanation for why whatever was in the house was so interested in the baby. No clue. This case was left completely unresolved."

Despite all the time and work she continued to put into the house in Deltona, she couldn't provide any answers. "There was nothing in any of the developers' blueprints or the local realtor reports. I talked to everybody. I was going nuts because there was no logical reason for the amount of activity that was going on in that house." By the time the husband moved out, the only explanation she was able to suggest was a half-hearted theory about the possibility of a prehistoric Indian burial ground. Though Dusty makes it clear that this was, at best, an educated guess, based on the fact that the area was once an Indian settlement. "Who knows?" she ultimately concludes. "They didn't exactly map sacred ground on colonial maps back then."

Another family moved in after the father left. Dusty came by once to leave her card with the new tenants; though she never heard from them, they only stayed three months. The house then sat empty for nine months, after which a single guy moved in. To Dusty's knowledge, this man still lives there.

"I used to date a gentleman that lived around there," Dusty says, "so I used to drive by the house fairly often. I did leave my card with the people next door, telling them if they had any problems they could give us a call. But we never heard anything."

The truth is, Dusty had problems letting the case go. "It became personal. We became like family to the victims, and even though I tried to remain emotionally removed from it, the things going on were so extreme that it was impossible to keep that objectivity. What made it even harder is we weren't able to give them any answers."

Out of a need to document the things that occurred in the Deltona home, and perhaps as a way to deal with the ultimate disappointment of not being able to come up with any answers, Dusty began to write a manuscript about the DBPRG's experiences there. The book was finished as of this writing, and if it hasn't managed to entirely exorcise the frustration Dusty still carries over the Deltona haunting, at least she's been able to turn it into a story—and quite a story at that.

Couldn't Clean Fast Enough

Maria Lopez doesn't live in Florida anymore, but the memories she has of the Sunshine State will likely stay with her forever—especially her memories of the house she cleaned for roughly two and half months in 1997. "I believe in spirits. Maybe I always believed in them," Maria says. "I come from a very old-fashioned, and maybe you could say superstitious, family. For my grandmother and my mother, there were dead people everywhere. I can remember the way they talked."

But then those otherworldly topics had been confined to her childhood, and when Maria moved to Orlando in 1997, decades had gone by without her giving the dead so much as a thought. "It was maybe, you could say, a hard time," she continues, surprisingly forthright. "I had a very young family, and we were working hard to put food on the table. Things are better now, thank God, but in Orlando, it was a lot of work."

For Maria, putting food on the table meant getting a job as a cleaning lady, and she was kept busy six days a week, nine hours a day, making her rounds through some of Orlando's finer homes, mopping floors, dusting furniture, cleaning drapes, beating rugs and similarly arduous work. "It was my first job in this country, and I was grateful for it," Maria says, "but the funny thing is that I don't remember a lot from those days. The houses were very nice houses, yes, but they were also all the same to me. Maybe they all represented something I could never afford."

But amid the haze of uniformly impressive abodes, one house stands out in Maria's memory. Or perhaps it would be more accurate to say that this was a house Mrs. Lopez will never be able to forget.

"You know, they seemed like a nice family. Most of the time they weren't there, and when they were, I spoke mostly to the mother. But they were normal people, it seemed to me. Two boys and one girl—they listened well to their mother. And the father was always smiling." And yet, from the very first time she walked into the house, Maria sensed that there was something wrong.

"I felt it almost right away," she says. "I wanted to make the sign of the cross when I walked inside for the very first time." But Maria resisted the urge to bless herself or display any fear in front of her new employers. "I tried to concentrate, you know, when the lady was showing me around, telling me what she wanted done, and her family was with her too, so I wanted to give them a good impression." Busy making sure that she was getting all her employer's instructions, Maria tried not to think too much about the weird feeling during her first few visits.

"Maybe it isn't such a nice thing to say," she says, "but it was a big and cold house, and there was no life in it. I told you they were nice people, but the house they lived in made me scared of them. I wondered, how can anyone live here?"

When asked what, exactly, she felt during the first few visits, Maria hesitates and her voice becomes uncertain. "I don't know what to say about that, but maybe the house felt angry." Maria pauses for a long moment before continuing. "I know that houses can't be angry, yes. But when I first walked into that house, I felt the same as if I were looking at someone who was very angry at me. I felt as if I was standing very close to someone who maybe wanted to hurt me. My heart, I remember, was beating hard, and I felt anxious. It didn't feel safe in that house."

Nevertheless, Maria had a young family to look after, and she didn't have the luxury of giving up jobs on hunches. Maria began her regular trips to the house that gave her the creeps. Once a week, every Friday morning, Maria would catch the bus to the house, unlock the door and go about her duties. It should have been an easy job. "These people paid me well," Maria explains, "and they didn't ask for too much work. I cleaned the floors and washed the bed sheets. I dusted their cabinets and tables in the living room, and cleaned all the bathrooms. Sometimes, the woman left extra work for me on a note in the kitchen, but always, she paid well for this."

The money wasn't an issue. In fact, it was one of the better paying jobs Maria had, which was why she stayed with it for as long as she did. As unsettling as she found the house during her first visits, the sense of foreboding only got worse—much worse—when she was there alone. "There was nowhere to go in the house that felt safe to me," she says. "Everything inside was wrong. I remember those old couches and chairs, the way they looked in the dark living room. It was scary, just very, very scary. Every time I was in the long hallway upstairs, the door to the master bedroom made me cold. I started to think about the things my mother and grandmother had told me a long time ago, about the dead people that walk around, but that we cannot see—ghosts."

On those Friday mornings, Maria found she couldn't work fast enough. Rushing through her duties, keeping her head down, barely daring to look around in case she might see something staring at her from across an empty room or down a long hallway. Not staring, rather, but glowering. Whatever was in the house, she knew beyond doubt that it was unfriendly.

But these were only feelings, impressions, and as long as the checks kept coming, Maria was willing to put up with them. It wasn't long, however, before her resolve was tested. "Most of the time, I just did my job and left, but sometimes there were notes left in the kitchen," she begins. "The first time I went to the basement, it was because of one of these notes. It said that there was extra detergent in the basement for cleaning the bathroom, if I ran out."

Maria claims that she was instantly uneasy about venturing downstairs. Being on the ground floor and the second floor was spooky enough, but the basement? The mere thought of it gave her shivers. "Yes, you could say I didn't want to do it at all," she says. "I felt for sure it was a bad idea."

But what could she do? She needed soap to clean the bathroom. "Maybe if they had heard all the bad things I was saying about them when I finally got the nerve to go downstairs, they wouldn't have wanted to hire me back," Maria laughs. "I wasn't happy about it. The lady was only asking for me to get soap, but it felt like she was trying to kill me."

Maria opened the basement door. The stairway was narrow and long, lit by a single naked bulb hanging from the ceiling. The room at the bottom of the stairs was dark. Wrestling with gut-churning fear, Maria's terror mounted with every step. "It wasn't like it was just a feeling anymore," she explains. "I *knew* someone was waiting for me, and I felt it was not a happy person. Downstairs was different from the rest of the house. The woman and her family didn't live there, I knew, but someone else did."

Maria makes it clear that this wasn't a living someone. No living person could live in the space she found at the bottom of the stairs. "When I turned the light on, I wanted to scream. Everything was upside down and all over the place. A loveseat was tipped over, the couch was upside down, boxes were scattered and a TV was sideways on a chair." It wasn't the disarray that frightened her, but the fact that it contrasted frightfully with the neatness upstairs and the thought that someone had *intentionally* upended the place in this way. There was far too much disorder for this to have occurred accidentally. Someone, some*thing*, was responsible for this.

And though she couldn't see what the something was, Maria was sure that it was in the room. The shadows seemed to be alive, looking at her, and panic drummed loudly in her chest. But she swallowed her fear and thought about her job. "All I knew for sure was that I had to get the soap. What was I going to say to them? 'Sorry, I couldn't clean the bathroom because I'm scared of your basement?'"

Luckily, the detergent was right by the stairs. Several bottles had fallen out of the box and were lying on the floor. "I picked up one of the bottles and ran upstairs as though I were being chased." When she got to the top, she slammed the door shut and locked it. "I knew what was wrong with the house now," says Maria. "There was something living in the basement, and the whole house felt wrong because of it."

Oddly, this knowledge made things somewhat easier for Maria. As creepy as the house was, she knew where the negative energy in the house came from. If she just stayed out of the basement, everything would be fine. Unfortunately, it wasn't going to be so easy.

The following Friday, there were no special instructions left in the kitchen; Maria came in, cleaned the house as fast as she could, and left without incident. But a week later, she found special instructions on the kitchen counter. "I think I almost cried when I saw the note," she says. "There was an old typewriter in one of their boys' rooms that they wanted me to take to the basement." Certainly a strange request; why didn't they move the typewriter themselves? But Maria wasn't of the mind to ask questions. She couldn't ignore the dread of what awaited her. Instead of rushing through her duties now, she was taking her time, putting off the inevitable descent for as long as she could.

"I take pride in my work, and I never break things or do a job halfway. This time, when I went to the basement, it was worse. He was waiting for me this time, and I felt in danger." When she's asked what made her certain that the something in the basement was a man, and how she knew she was in danger, Maria isn't sure how to respond. "It's true, I couldn't see him, but I still knew. I knew he was a man, a dead man, and that if he could, he would hurt me."

It wasn't a pleasant thing to know, and Maria wasn't downstairs a moment longer than she needed to be. "I didn't even go all the way down," she says. "I was still on the stairs, I didn't even turn on the lights and I threw the type-writer into the room. It crashed when it hit the ground. Maybe I broke it, but I didn't care, and I ran upstairs and locked the door."

After that, the job became increasingly worse with each passing week. Every Friday, Maria discovered notes in the kitchen asking her to put something or another in the basement for storage, or bring something up. And each time she ventured down, the foreboding feeling increased. "You know, I knew what was happening. They were all scared of going to their own basement, that's why it was such a disaster downstairs. Maybe that's even why they hired me in the first place. They needed someone to take things back and forth."

A solid enough theory, but it didn't stop Maria from doing as she was told. They were paying her, after all. But even a hard worker like Maria Lopez had her limits, and after two and a half months of dealing with the Orlando family's ghost, she reached her breaking point.

The day began the same way it had for weeks—with a note sitting on the kitchen counter instructing Maria to make a foray into the basement. This request was different from the others, though. "Before, whenever they had asked me to get something from the basement, it was always something like soap or sponges or toilet paper…stuff like that. You know, cleaning supplies, things I know they stored in the basement just by throwing them down the stairs."

According to Maria, these things were always piled up around the bottom of the stairs, so she was never required to venture too far. This time, however, the note asked her for something else. "Maybe I was more mad than scared when I read that note," she says. "This woman's husband needed a box of books for his work room upstairs. The note said not to worry; it was a small box! She wanted me to find a box in that disaster downstairs—a *small* box!" To make matters worse, Maria was told that the books were not in the room at the bottom of the stairs, but in another room down the hall. Until then, she'd never taken more than two steps away from the staircase, and even then she was having a difficult enough time coping with the waves of fear that rolled over her. The thought of walking *into* the basement caused her to reconsider her working arrangement.

Incredibly though, Maria went about cleaning the house, all the while steeling herself for the ordeal in the basement. "Everyone always tells me how stubborn I am," Maria says. "My mother used to say it, my brothers, my husband. Always, 'Maria, you're so stubborn!' I think maybe they're right. Because I was going to go down and find that box of books for that cowardly man who was too scared to go down to the basement himself."

Only after she was sure that everything was in its rightful place on the first and second floors did she ready herself for the descent into the chaotic basement. Maria said a prayer, made the sign of the cross and went downstairs. Though the walk down to the basement had become familiar by now, the sight of the dark room below still filled her with as much terror as it had the first time.

She made her way down slowly, each hesitant step a major effort. Halfway down, the instinct to turn and run was threatening to overwhelm her. She could make out the discarded couches and chair in the darkness. The television set, the knocked-over boxes. Her eyes drifted involuntarily to the black corners, and the now-familiar sense that a hostile man was lurking there sent a cold spasm down her back. Still, she continued until she got to the bottom of the stairs, where she stopped to flip the light switch.

The light flickered from a single bulb that hung naked from the ceiling. "The light made it worse," she says. "There was broken glass and stains on the floor. The light was dim, and it was very quiet. I could hear my heart, and I didn't want to go any farther. I wanted to run."

But her stubbornness beat out her fear. Noticing the hallway that led out of the devastated rumpus room, she fought down the inexplicable terror welling inside and took her first step forward. "Maybe I had walked a few feet to the hallway when the TV fell off the chair—by itself, just like that. I was so scared that the crash made me jump and scream." And run.

"My feet went by themselves," Maria continues. "I couldn't stay down there for too long because I felt that I might have a heart attack. I ran to the room where they told me the books were." Yet as soon as she started to run, she was overcome with the feeling that she was being chased. "He liked that I was scared. I know it," she says. "When I was in the hallway, I heard something else smash behind me. It was closer than the TV. Then there was something even closer. He was coming."

Not risking a glance back, Maria ran to the door, opened it and then slammed it shut behind her. "The room looked as though it had been used as a place for the man to sit and read," Maria says. "There were shelves on the walls, but all the books were on the floor, and there was a broken rocking chair, and one stuffed chair laying on its side. I tried to turn on the light, but there was nothing. It was broken. There was only a little bit of light from a small window, covered by weeds on the outside."

Still, there was just enough light to see, and Maria recognized the small box that had been described in the note. "I took that damned box and was going to run out, but thought, *no*, when I got to the door." Box of books in one arm, she refused to turn the handle.

"He was waiting for me on the other side of the door. I could hear him." Maria's manner, which has until now been generally vivacious, darkens considerably. She is almost whispering when she continues. "He was laughing. I could hear him laughing on the other side of the door." She describes it as more of a chuckle, actually—low and throaty, and unequivocally malicious. Yet Maria didn't scream. No. She began to shout.

"I couldn't open the door. I was too scared. I didn't want to see him. But I shouted at him. I swore at him in Spanish and English. I called him a coward, trying to scare me when I was alone and trying to finish a job so that I could feed my kids." This strategy didn't seem to work.

She could hear the heavy crashes from the next room. The bookshelves on the adjacent wall shook and rattled with every crash. Every time something was thrown, Maria jumped. "Well, I didn't know what to do," she says. "I was so scared. I didn't know what he was capable of. Maybe anything. He had a lot of hate, and he was unhappy I was there."

It sounded as though the room down the hall was being trashed, but the little study Maria had locked herself in felt relatively safe. It didn't have the same chill as the trashed rumpus room; this room felt secure. She didn't allow herself to think about going out and facing the angry spirit.

She remained pressed against the door, the box of books in her arms. "I don't know how long I was there," she says. "But I think it was a while. I was starting to wonder if I'd be in there all day when the noise stopped." According to Maria, it had stopped suddenly. One moment, all hell was breaking loose, the next—nothing.

The silence didn't take the edge off Maria's fear, however; if anything, it made it worse. The silence seemed more threatening. She was convinced he was waiting, just outside the door. "Besides what I heard from my mother and my grandmother, I didn't know anything about ghosts. I didn't know what this man might do, but I knew that I was scared, and that there was no way I was going to open that door." But then, in the next instant, she couldn't get it open fast enough.

"After that day, I knew that in hell, it isn't hot. It's cold. The devil doesn't like fire. He keeps it very, very cold." Maria's conclusion is based on what transpired only seconds after the banging ceased in the rec room. A cold passed through her, so sudden and intense that for several seconds she was unable to breathe. The whole room became extremely cold, and Maria knew she wasn't alone.

Her every instinct told her to throw open the door and run, but she found herself turning, moved by a curiosity that she could not ignore. "I saw him. He was in the room, a few feet behind me. He was just a shadow. I couldn't see his face, his body, nothing. He was all black, like a shadow."

Maria didn't stick around for closer observation; she turned and ran. "I don't know if he was chasing me or not. I didn't notice anything. I went straight up the stairs and locked the door. I put those stupid books in the workroom upstairs, and I was finished. I never went back to that house again."

Today, Maria is certain beyond any doubt that the Orlando family hired her mainly because they were too frightened to go to their own basement themselves. Once she demonstrated that she was willing to venture into the rec room, the requests to run little errands into the basement became a weekly occurrence.

As for who the ghost may have been, and why the family chose to continue living there, Maria has no idea. "You know, I think about that family sometimes," Maria says. "Now, when I think of it, the family seemed spookier to me than the ghost in their basement. How could they live like that? Why didn't they move? Those people were so *weird.*"

What about the dead man? Her opinions on the black figure that she saw in the basement study? "I didn't pay much attention to the stories when my grandmother and my mother would talk about ghosts," Maria responds, "but I remember the stories about the dead people were always a mystery. *El misterio.* 'Don't think too much about the dead people,' my grandmother would say. 'If you do, you'll go crazy.' Now I know what she means."

Nothing on TV

"The truth is, most people are so bound by what they will and won't allow themselves to believe that they can't see most of the world in front of them. Most people are living like moles in their little holes." Stephen Webb, a pseudonym, is nothing if not opinionated, and in one discussion with this Miami man, it was made clear how truly off-center some opinions can be.

"The dead are everywhere. It's a fact," he insists, sounding like a television attorney talking to a jury. "And no amount of snorting, rolling of eyes or ballyhooing about it is going to change that fact. We may want to tell ourselves different. But we may as well face it—the dead aren't going anywhere. And if they're pissed off, they're going to let you know about it."

After a few minutes of conversation with Stephen, it is obvious he has a story he wants to tell, and yet on the same note, he's adamant about keeping his name from print. "Believe me," he says, "after what I've been through, the last thing I want is more people spouting off their opinions on how I'm nuts or I'm desperate for attention. No thanks. I learned my lesson. The fewer people who know about it, the better."

Not that "Stephen Webb" was always so wary about attaching his name to a ghost story. In fact, before his experiences in his former Miami home several years ago, he didn't have an opinion about ghosts at all. "It wasn't that I believed in them or didn't believe in them," he says. "Just like most people, I didn't really give a damn. You know, ghosts were for the movies, and that was that. But don't think that I would have ever laughed at somebody or called them crazy if they told me they saw one. That's not my style. If someone has a story, and they're serious about it, you listen—simple as that." Admirable, perhaps, but in 1999, Stephen discovered that when it came time to consider the supernatural, very few people shared this attitude.

"I had just gotten a raise and moved into a new place in West Miramar. Single story concrete place—nothing special. But one hell of a step up from the bachelor pad hellhole I was living in before." It wouldn't be long, however, before events in his new bungalow would make Stephen look back fondly on his time in his "bachelor pad hellhole."

"Well, it was just past a week in when I got my first hint that something was screwy in my new place," Stephen continues. "I'm a pretty regular guy. I've got my routines, and one of 'em is to sit down and watch a bit of tube for an hour or so after work. Problem is, you need a remote to watch TV, and that day, I couldn't find my damn remote anywhere."

"You need to know me to know how weird that is," Stephen says. "Like I said, I've got my routines. My remote never leaves the armrest of my chair. Never. That's where I put it. That's where it has always been. End of story. But this day, it was missing.

Stephen tore his house apart that day. He checked under the cushions, under couches and chairs, behind the television. Did he accidentally take it to the bathroom? He searched in the medicine cabinet, the sink drawers, in the shower, even behind the toilet. No. In the kitchen? He opened up all the kitchen cupboards, dug through the cutlery, inspected the sink, the fridge, the freezer. No remote in sight. He searched his room, the second bedroom, the closet, the backyard. Nothing.

"I spent my whole night looking for the thing, and it was nowhere. I'd started looking at around seven, and I was still searching after nine. I knew there was no way I had misplaced the thing, and I started to think that someone must have broken in and stolen it." Stephen pauses for a long moment and then chuckles. "I know. Who the hell would break into a guy's place, leave the TV and steal the remote? Makes no sense. But it was the only thing I could think of."

Stephen went to bed fuming that night, and he woke up the next morning with one thing on his mind: his remote. "It was all I could think about the whole time I was at work. On my way home, I picked up a new one and another lock for my door. The lock went up first, then I put the remote on the armrest where it belonged."

His TV time was pushed back about two hours that night, but after installing the chain on his door and digging a beer out of the fridge, he was ready to enjoy his down-time all the same. He cracked open his can of beer, picked up the remote and hit the power button. But... "the damn thing didn't turn on! Okay. I was mad now. I thought first it was the remote, and I knocked the thing around a bit. I tried it again, but still nothing."

Conceding ultimate defeat to his remote, Stephen got up, walked to the television, and hit the power button. Remote or no remote, he was watching some TV. Or so he

thought. "It was like I was in the Twilight Zone or something. The thing wouldn't turn on! I hit the button so
many times I thought I might punch a hole through it!
First the remote vanishes, now the TV wasn't working.
I couldn't understand what was going on."

And so it was that, other than the constant string of
epithets Stephen directed at his television set, a second
night at the Webb household was spent in silence. "Next
morning, I loaded the TV into my car and took it to be
fixed after work; they told me to come back in two days."

Stephen twiddled his thumbs for the next two evenings
until it was time to go to sleep, not knowing that his frustrated boredom was about to be punctuated by the most
frightening experience of his life. "I still remember exactly
what time it was. My alarm clock read 2:53 AM. I think my
first thought was that I was dreaming."

Silver light was flickering down the hallway and
through his open doorway. He stared out the window for
several uncomprehending seconds before sitting up on his
elbows. The light was still there. "I remember thinking,
what the hell? I was definitely a bit freaked out, too. At
first, I thought some punk had broken into my place, but
then that didn't make any sense. What was with the light?
I looked at my clock again. It was exactly 2:55. I took my
baseball bat out of my closet and went out to see what was
going on."

Only when he was in the hallway, walking to his living
room, did it occur to him what the glimmering light
might be. "It made even less sense than everything that
had been going on, but it hit me then that there was only
one thing it could be. Static from a TV—I knew it was

impossible. There was no TV in the room. But, at the same time, I knew it could be nothing else. There was a TV turned on in the living room."

As strange as the idea of someone breaking into his house in the middle of the night to deposit a television set was, the sight that greeted Stephen when he walked into the room was even more incomprehensible. "There was nothing there. The whole room was lit up like a TV running static, but there was no TV. The light was flashing, it was filling up the room, but there was no source."

Stephen reached for the light switch then, but before his hand found the switch, his eyes fell on something that made his blood run cold. There, on the armrest of his chair, were two remote controls—the one he'd just bought lying atop the one he thought he'd lost. "Yeah," he says with a chuckle, "that is when I knew that something extremely screwed up was happening. The crazy scared feeling up my back was telling me more than my head could. A ghost. When I hit the light and the TV static vanished, I knew that my new house had a ghost."

But although Stephen was ready to accept this, he was somewhat surprised at how unwilling everybody was to take him seriously. "Some people call me a loud mouth, and it's true that I'm the kind of guy that calls it like he sees it. I've got no use for lies or secrets, and I pretty well say what's on my mind. If I have got an issue, people usually know about it."

This philosophy may have worked fine for Stephen most of the time, but he was about to discover that it wasn't nearly as effective when his issue involved a vanishing remote control and a phantom television set. "The guys at work all thought I was joking at first, and then when I pushed it some of them thought I'd cracked. They blamed it on the heat or on all the concrete," he laughs, "two things that Miramar has no shortage of."

Undeterred by the reactions he'd faced that day, he met his two best friends for drinks that night. "Well, these two jokers thought it was the funniest thing they'd ever heard. Started making cracks about how I'd never spent a night away from my TV, and that it was just me missing the 'ol' gal,' and ridiculous statements like that. It was incredible. No one was taking me seriously," Stephen recalls.

In a way, given the nature of his story, it seems just as incredible that Stephen would expect people to take his tale seriously, but apparently, he held his own word at higher value than his friends and associates. His truth had become everyone else's nonsense. Stephen says he underwent a major change in his personal philosophy after his experience, and decided that there were times when telling the truth for truth's sake wasn't the best way to go.

Anyway, all the truth telling in the world wasn't going to make the following night any easier. "It wasn't the most comfortable feeling when I got home. I didn't have any weird feelings, or *premonitions,* as some people call them, but I couldn't shake the feeling that there was someone else in the house with me. I didn't have my TV back yet, and so I drove myself crazy wondering whether or not I was being watched."

Those kinds of thoughts might easily keep someone up all night, jumping at the sound of the clicks and bangs of the air conditioner, but in Stephen's case, sheer exhaustion eventually took over. He hadn't slept well the night before, and no amount of fear could keep his eyes open past midnight.

But sure enough, his eyes flicked open almost three hours later because of the muted silver light flickering down the hallway. "The second night, it hit me harder," Stephen says. "This meant that the night before wasn't an isolated incident, and that there really was something in my house that I had no control over. But what really got to me that night was the thing, the *mist*, that came into my room."

According to Stephen, it appeared as he sat there in his bed, heart pounding, trying to steel the courage to get up and investigate. "I think I was just about to get out of bed when it appeared at the door. It was a big, vaporous fog, about the size of a person, and glowing silver in the light from the hall," Stephen says. "Later on, I learned through research that this thing was an ectoplasmic mist—the gas form of a paranormal energy—but that night, all I saw was a cloud of vapor that looked alive, one that felt like it could *see* me, and was coming into my room."

The moment it entered, the temperature in Stephen's bedroom plummeted, and even as he went for his baseball bat, he knew that no amount of swinging would affect the thing that had just drifted into his room. "I wanted to get up and switch the lights on," Stephen says. "It sounds weird, but I just knew that if I got out of bed, ran past this thing and hit the lights, that it would vanish." Unfortunately, though, this was easier said than done.

"As much as I wanted to jump off the bed, I couldn't. I may as well have been glued to the mattress. I wanted to, but my body wouldn't move. I guess I didn't have the guts to run past this thing. I didn't want to make any sudden movements around it, and going to the lights meant I'd have to get way too close."

Still, while Webb wasn't at all eager to get any closer to the roiling mass of silver mist, closer seemed to be exactly what the mist had in mind; it drifted toward him while he sat paralyzed by fear. "What finally snapped me out of it was this loud sound," Stephen continues. "It was the sound of static like a television stuck on a dead channel, and loud, as though there was a TV on full blast in my room."

Once he had snapped out of his terrified trance, Stephen jumped from his bed and lunged across the room. His hunch had been right. The moment he hit the lights, the mist vanished, the silver light went out and the sound of static quit. He was alone in the sudden quiet of his room.

"I figured that one way to keep this TV ghost, or whatever it was, from coming into my room again was to keep the light on." The light stayed on for the rest of the night, and Stephen tossed and turned, unable to put his mind at rest after what he had just experienced.

"The next day was hell. I was tired, and I made the mistake of telling a few of my closer coworkers about what happened. They took me a lot more seriously the second time around. I was looking really rough, I guess, and one of my friends at work got worried. I'm pretty sure he was the one who told my boss about it, and I was called into the man's office after lunch. He was good about it. He asked me how I was doing, said that I looked really tired and that some of the guys were worried about me. He told me that I should take the rest of the day off, rest up, come back with a clear head in the morning."

Clocking out after half a day, Stephen came to the decision then and there that work was no place to discuss his ghostly experiences, and no one in his place of employment would hear another word. "I wasn't in the best frame of mind when I dropped by the electronic store to pick up my TV. They told me nothing was wrong with the thing—surprise, surprise. They turned it on right in front of me and suggested that maybe there had been a power-out when I tried to turn it on."

Such a suggestion was not effective in putting Stephen's mind at ease. He felt that he might be going crazy. "When I got home, I plugged in the TV. But then…" Stephen hesitated before continuing. "I just sat there looking at the screen. I couldn't get myself to do it. I didn't know what would happen if I tried to turn it on. I'm telling you, I had the remote in my hand, and my thumb on the power button, but I just couldn't push the button. Whatever this thing was, it had me right spooked. And that was when it hit me: *alright, I've got to get some help with this situation.*"

Help? Where does one go to get help with ghosts?

"I have never really been a religious type of guy," Stephen says. "I was baptized when I was a kid, but except for a couple of weddings and one funeral, I've never really been to church." And yet incredibly, two days in his new place had Stephen dwelling on the divine. "So, I visited a church to ask for some help. What do I know, right? Heaven and hell…the afterlife—I thought someone there might have something to say about what was going on."

Sadly, Stephen found no more sympathy at his nearest church than he did at work. The pastor wasn't able to give him any satisfactory answers. "I went with what I thought were some pretty specific questions, but the pastor only talked about my personal demons, how they can come in the form of nightmares, addictions, rage, and that personal demons can sometimes make a guy see things that aren't there. He suggested that the problem was *me*. Like *I* was guilty of something, *I* was responsible for what I was seeing. He made it sound like none of this was even happening, that my *personal demons* were driving me crazy, and I was imagining this stuff. I couldn't believe it. Not even a priest would take me seriously."

Unwilling to go home and be alone with his television set, Stephen drove around for most of the afternoon, thinking of every possible errand he could run to keep himself busy. "It was pretty funny. I went out and bought food. Picked up a few books and magazines. Took a look at stereo equipment. I wasn't interested in buying—just doing anything to stay out of the house."

Eventually, inevitably, he had to go back home, and the first thing his eyes fell on when he opened the door was the big black television, looming there in his living room. "I made myself some dinner and I read my magazines. After that, I locked myself in my room and started reading one of the books I bought," he says. "The amazing thing was that I managed to forget about it, and after about an hour or so of reading, I could no longer keep my eyes open and ended up passing out with my clothes on."

If Stephen dared to hope that cracking open a book was all it would take to get rid of the television-obsessed spirit haunting his home, he was sorely mistaken. When he was woken in the middle of the night by the sound of static coming from the living room, he was hardly caught unawares. "I got up and turned my bedroom light off, and sure enough, there was the blue light shining underneath my closed door."

A strange thing happened then. Suddenly, Stephen Webb found himself more irritated than he was scared. "At this point, I was angry. It would be the third night in a row with very little sleep," he says, now laughing. "This *thing*, whatever this *thing* was, wasn't paying a *cent* for the rent, and had the gall to be keeping me up like this? I don't think so."

With these thoughts buzzing around in his head like a hive of angry bees, Stephen threw open the door and charged into the living room. Sure enough, the television was on with its blank screen buzzing, the room full of static and flickering blue light. "Well, this is going to sound crazy, but by this time, I pretty well was crazy," he says. I grabbed the cord and pulled it out of the wall, hauled the TV up on my shoulder, kicked open the door hauled it out to the front yard and threw it to the curb. I walked back inside, grabbed the remote controls and threw them out onto the street, too."

Stephen went to bed that night and slept quite peacefully through the rest of the night, all things considered. "By the time I got up for work the next morning, someone had already cleared the TV away. The guys at work were on me for most of the day about all the stuff I'd said the last two days, but I turned the story around, telling them I couldn't believe they all fell for it, and that at least I got a day off out of the whole deal."

That afternoon, Stephen sat down in his living room and resumed the book he'd been reading the night before. "It's weird that I'd feel so good about the situation. I'd just lost my TV and had nothing to do to kill the rest of the day, but what can I say? I guess it must have been a good book."

And there would be a lot of good books to follow. Even though the strange phenomenon in his living room ceased its late-night torments from then on, Stephen abandoned television for books as his favorite pastime. He never bothered picking up another television set, and he took to visiting bookstores on a regular basis. He claims to have accumulated quite the little library. More than a few of the books on his shelves deal with ghosts and other inexplicable phenomenon.

"I've been spending a lot of time trying to figure out what happened in my house for those three nights," Stephen says. "A lot of my reading has been about paranormal phenomena." But the now-avid reader claims he hasn't had much luck in coming up with any definitive answers. To this day, all he's able to provide is speculation.

"I know it couldn't have been my TV on its own," he says. "I used the thing for years without any problems before I moved into the new place. But what I've been trying to figure out is why it stopped after I tossed my television. It doesn't make any sense to me at all."

Nevertheless, Stephen swears that every word of it happened, that the incidents were neither freakish dreams nor a play for a day off. "As crazy as those three nights were," Stephen says, "thinking back, I am amazed at how totally unwilling everybody was to believe a word of what I was saying. You start telling people you've seen a ghost, and they'd rather call you a liar or a joker or a nut than even consider taking you seriously. It was a real wake-up call. Goes to show there are some things you just can't talk about."

3
Haunted Landscapes

The Ghostly Folklore
of Escambia County

Escambia—an undeniably exotic name, better suited, perhaps, to some fantastical fairytale realm rather than the county on Florida's western border. But then again, maybe the handle is a fitting one. No one has seen any white-spired castles, knights errant in search of damsels in distress, or houses made of cake and candy there, but the faraway county on the far end of the state's panhandle has stories of its own—some uncanny enough to compete with anything ever written by the Brothers Grimm.

Escambia County's history alone sets it apart from most other places in the United States. The land around Pensacola Bay was the first site of European colonization in North America, preceding the Pilgrims' arrival at Plymouth by over 60 years. The Viceroy of New Spain, Luis de Velasco, was the one who chose Pensacola Bay for this historic settlement. A historic settlement, yes, but initially not a successful one.

The first colonists who arrived on August 15, 1559, were hit by a hurricane 35 later. Many of them died and all but three of the ships anchored in the bay were sunk. This first colony would never recover from this setback. Fear and hunger among the settlers sparked fires of mutiny, and they retreated back to Mexico a mere two years after they arrived. This was only the beginning of a long and eventful history, which would eventually see five different flags fly over the Pensacola colony.

After the return of the Spanish over 100 years later in 1698, the colony passed from the Spanish to the French, back to the Spanish, to the British, and then back into the possession of the Spanish. It wasn't until 1821, over 250 years after the initial settlement, that Florida became a territory of the United States—Escambia was its first county, and future president Andrew Jackson, its first governor. Yet, this didn't mark the end of Pensacola's penchant for flag swapping.

Spain. France. Britain. The United States—only four flags. The fifth was the Stars and Bars, raised over Pensacola Bay in 1861, when Confederate soldiers took over Fort McRee during the Civil War. One year later, Union troops took it back, and so it stands to this day, with the sobriquet "City of the Five Flags," a reminder of the area's turbulent history.

With this chaotic backdrop of hurricanes and switching allegiances, Escambia County became a storied region, full of bizarre tales involving Spanish soldiers, swooning Indian maidens, angry Indian fathers and the ghosts these dramas bred. Throw in a swamp-dwelling, southern bigfoot called the Skunkape, and you've got a rough outline of the folklore of this dramatic little corner of Florida.

The Lone Spaniard

Juan Alverado was a Spanish soldier who'd been stationed in Cuba before his unit was moved to the swamps of Escambia. He was assigned to an outfit that was ordered to accompany an exploration party set to map out the course of the Escambia River in preparation for an approaching road-building crew. This is all that is really known about Alverado's background. He was a soldier with a job to do.

He was also a soldier who ended up in the wrong place at the wrong time. Fate dealt its hand to Juan the morning he and a fellow soldier received orders to accompany two Indian guides along the banks of the river. They were to report back to their unit that night with a detailed account of what they'd seen—an order neither men would fulfill.

The details about the Indians are even sketchier than they are on the two Spaniards who disappeared with them that day. What is known is that there existed two main tribes in the region at the time: the Creek and the Poarch. It isn't known for certain what tribe this pair belonged to, nor why they schemed such a nefarious plan.

Then again, it can't even be said if the violence that erupted between the Spaniards and the Indians was pre-meditated. It may have resulted from an unintentional insult. Perhaps it began as a disagreement over directions. Or maybe the Spaniards initiated the violence. Who knows? They may have been plotting desertion and saw the two Indians as an obstacle. It is impossible to say for certain, and the legend doesn't provide an explanation.

What the legend *does* tell us is that a fight to the death erupted between the soldiers and the Indians, and that the Spaniards didn't fare well. Alverado's companion was killed in the struggle, and Alvarado was gravely wounded. And yet he managed to make his escape. After cutting one of his assailants badly, he lunged into the forest, leaving the one Indian to look after his wounded comrade. Alverado ran as fast and as far as he could, but it wasn't long before his wound began to take its toll. His run slowed to a painful lurch, his uniform was saturated with blood and sweat.

Behind him, he could hear the two Indians. The man he'd wounded was on his feet again, and they were coming after him. He knew he wouldn't stand a chance in a fight, and as he felt himself growing weaker and weaker with every step, he knew he wouldn't be able to outrun them. It was then that he spotted the big cypress tree with a hollow in the trunk.

Wincing in pain, Alverado crouched low and crawled into the hollow. There he waited, hidden from sight as the two Indians ran past, missing him entirely. There he remained, feeling his lifeblood seep out from under his breastplate, down his arms and legs and into the ground.

Of course, this isn't the end of the story. Not long after the confrontation, the local Indians began to speak of a strange thing in the woods. The vision always material- ized around sunset—a transparent man, white as death, dressed in Spanish armor, walking the woods as the sun dipped out of sight and dusk darkened the forest. One look at this man in steel would cause a coldness to creep up the back, and fill one's heart with fear.

The Indians were quick to make the connections. After all, they knew about the attack on the two soldiers, and they declared this the spirit of one of the Spaniards, the one who had been killed at the hands of his assailant, assuming Alverado had evaded the Indians and made his escape. They learned to give the dead man distance, respecting the restless spirit's need to wander, and the lone apparition became a fixture of the lower Escambia River.

Eventually, word of the ghost in the woods spread from the local Indians to the nonnatives in the region. The story of the two soldiers and their demise at the hands of their guides was eventually passed on to the Spanish, who, in time, would pass it on to the English settlers. Years became decades and then centuries, and still the lone Spanish soldier continued to appear—drifting through the woods at sunset, dressed in his now anachronistic armor, a hollow look in his lifeless eyes.

The only name that survived in subsequent tellings of the tale was Juan Alverado. In the telling, he was the man who had eluded death, the one who escaped the bloody hatchets of his pursuers. But escaped to where? No one could say for certain. Only that Alverado was the survivor. The ghost belonged to the other, less fortunate man. Then, in the late 1920s, a grisly discovery near the Escambia River revealed the not-so-fortunate fate of the man who had presumably survived.

Loggers eventually found him. The local lumber industry was kicking into high gear, and loggers were all over the county, cutting down every tree in sight. One of those trees was a big old cypress tree near the banks of the Escambia. According to legend, the tree split open and let out a terrible groan when it was felled. And there, inside the hollowed out trunk, was a skeleton dressed in Spanish armor. Juan Alverado had been found at last. He'd only escaped far enough to find his verdant tomb. The lucky soldier hadn't been so lucky after all.

Yet it wasn't until the skeleton was given a proper burial in a Pensacola cemetery that people began linking the ghost of the lone Spaniard with the body found in the tree. For after the bones were interred, the spirit of the solitary Spaniard stopped appearing before startled Floridians. Years went by without a sign of the dead man in the Spanish armor, and the tale was revised. It wasn't the ghost of Juan Alverado's companion that had wandered the area for all those centuries, but the restless spirit of Alverado himself.

And so the unfortunate soldier hadn't escaped, but rather imprisoned himself. For centuries, his restless spirit was tied to the body that lay within the living tomb of the cypress tree. Only after the tree had been cut down and Juan Alverado given a proper burial was his spirit set free and allowed to rest.

The Legend of Green Pine Stump

What are the chances? One Spanish soldier named Juan Alverado is attacked and mortally wounded by an Indian guide, and around the same time another Spanish soldier named Juan falls a foul to a local Indian chief for a romantic tryst with his daughter—both around the same region. Apparently, it was a bad year for men named Juan in Escambia.

At around the same time as Juan Alverado was accompanying an expedition up the Escambia River, the Juan of this tale was part of another military escort sent out with a group to explore the shores of Escambia Bay. The story begins the morning Juan went foraging through the woods with hopes of finding wild game. He was unfamiliar with the country and promptly lost his way in the dense woodland.

Loaded with weapons and armor and fighting off panic, Juan would have stumbled around the hot and humid woodland for some time had he not run into a young woman out enjoying a casual stroll. Given the eventual outcome of their meeting, it would have been best if Juan had never laid eyes on this woman at all, but when he first saw her, he couldn't comprehend her as anything but a blessing.

As is usually the case with star-crossed couples, it was love at first sight. Napeese, the chief's daughter, was as beautiful and desirable to Juan as she was with her tribe. This lone, lost Spaniard took instant possession of her heart.

It was obvious Juan was lost, and Napeese led him back to her settlement where he ended up spending the night. Because it was her people's way, Juan was greeted with hospitality, but it was easy to see that no one was very happy with the arrival of the young stranger. They worried for Napeese, who seemed completely transfixed by her guest. Everyone smelled trouble.

Trouble came when Napeese's father got wind of the situation and came storming down to see what was going on. His daughter's infatuation was as obvious to him as it was to everyone else, and he ordered that Juan be led out of the village and back to his people immediately.

Napeese was allowed to accompany Juan and his escort. While walking back through the trees the way they came, they cast sorrowful glances at one another when they passed the place where they had met. A few hours later, the sight of Juan's camp filled the soldier with sadness. The time had come to split with Napeese.

As the chief's daughter, Napeese didn't allow herself to display too much emotion in front of the men of her village, but Juan could see how unhappy she was. They embraced, and when they did, Juan whispered that he would go back to the place where they met the next day, and the next day after that. He would continue to go there until he saw her again.

Of course, Napeese didn't speak Spanish, but there was a bond between the two, and for those who know anything about tragic love, words are unnecessary between pairings such as this. All that was required was a single look, and Napeese understood. She would see Juan at the meeting place tomorrow.

They met the next day, and the day after that. They met in secret—Juan stealing away from his camp, forsaking whatever military duties he'd been assigned, Napeese dodging the ever-watchful eye of her father. Details about what the pair did when they met probably aren't necessary, but each time, they found it harder and harder to go their separate ways, and their outings grew longer with every meeting.

Soon, Juan went about the task of building a shelter that would accommodate their ever-lengthening stays, and he had a serviceable pine cabin standing before long. The roof over their heads only encouraged their trysts, and it became common for them to spend entire days in one another's company.

This wasn't too much of a problem for Juan, who was enjoying a lax command at his camp on the shoreline, but Napeese was foolish in allowing herself to believe that she wasn't being missed. She was, after all, the tribe's favorite daughter, and the eyes of her people followed her wherever she went. The common assumption was that she was going out to meet with the Spanish soldier, and, of course, the assumption was right. But one man didn't even allow himself to consider it, and no one dared to bring the affair to his attention.

Napeese's father had such fierce confidence in his daughter's obedience that he assumed that she would obey him without question. For him, it wasn't a possibility that she would go against his word. But he realized this confidence was being tested. As firm as his faith was in Napeese, his eyes were telling him a different story. The chief was watchful and intelligent, and he took note of his daughter's extended absences.

One day, he confronted her about it. "Daughter," he said with a voice that was both affectionate and severe. "I have noticed that you spend a great deal of time away from home. Sometimes you are gone from sunup to sundown. What are you doing, out among the trees, that takes up so much of your days?"

Napeese looked at her father with the sweetest expression she could muster, and when she spoke, tried to imagine that her father meant Juan, when he asked about the trees. "I go out among the trees because they are home to me, father. It is only when I'm in their shade that I feel at ease." This was enough for the chief, who wasn't accustomed to doubting the words of his daughter, and he did his best to forget the matter.

Yet no matter how he tried, he couldn't stop the worm of doubt from creeping into his mind. Now, Napeese was coming home well after the sun had gone down, and though he did his best to ignore them, he was aware of the whispers among the villagers. He knew what they were saying about his daughter and the Spaniard. No one, however, would say it to his face, fearing what might happen to them, as well as what might happen to Napeese if such suspicions were confirmed.

There is no way of knowing what the chief was thinking when he decided to follow his daughter out one morning. Had he finally convinced himself that she was indeed seeing the Spaniard against his wishes? Was he following her in a seething rage? Or was he going out only to put his mind at ease, aiming to convince himself that whatever doubts he had were unwarranted, and that his daughter was doing no wrong?

At first, it may have appeared as though Napeese had been truthful. Watching his daughter from a safe distance as she skipped through the woods, the chief couldn't help but notice that she seemed truly at peace under the forest's boughs. She went along with a broad smile, running her hands across branches, singing a silent song that was meant only for herself. Perhaps if Juan's cabin had been only a little bit further away, the chief may have turned away without seeing it, convinced that Napeese truly was a daughter of the wood. But this wasn't the case. His blood froze when the cabin came into sight; there stood the young man his daughter had brought back to tribe that day—the Spaniard, the same man she had been forbidden to see.

For as long as people have been around, all sorts of brutal acts have been committed in moments when human reason is overcome by violent emotion. The day that Napeese's father witnessed his daughter's betrayal in the woods near Escambia Bay, another such act was committed. At least, in this instance, there would be something poetic about it.

Napeese and Juan turned their backs and walked into the cabin as the chief ran from his cover, unslinging his bow and notching an arrow. They were embracing inside when he barged through the door and let his arrow fly, killing both of them. They fell to the ground of their little pine cabin, stapled to one another by the single arrow that pierced both their hearts. The chief turned his back on them then, walked back to his village and ordered his warriors to go into the woods and burn down the pine cabin.

Just another soldier lost in the colonies, Juan was quickly forgotten by the Spanish, but Napeese was another story. Though no one was permitted to talk about what had happened in the chief's presence, Napeese's murder affected everyone, and the village never quite recovered from her death.

It did not help that, for years afterward, many people claimed to have spotted Napeese and Juan standing in the place where they were killed. They were only ever seen in the early morning, usually by startled hunters heading out in search of game. Both looked real enough—the light glinting off Juan's armor, the brilliant smile on Napeese's face—but the fact that they were completely transparent ensured that no one who saw the pair would mistake them for living people. No one was able to get closer than 20 feet or so before the couple would vanish into thin air. But not without leaving something behind.

A pine tree stump remained from one of the trees that Juan had cut down while constructing their cabin. Indians from Napeese's tribe soon noticed that, though the clearing was charred and burnt from the cabin fire, this lone stump was still green, sprouting leaves and branches when it ought to have been lifeless. Many of the villagers took this as a sign of Napeese's spirit; the apparitions were always seen near the green stump.

It is said that the two apparitions only ceased appearing years later, when the Indians in the area were vacated from their lands. Even then, the more observant among the American settlers noticed the pine stump, which was still as green as ever, the last reminder of Juan and Napeese.

The Dreaded Skunkape:
Bigfoot of the South

If he does exist, there is no telling how old he would be by now and the odds are that no one, not even the most passionate zoologists, would care to get close enough to find out. He's called the Skunkape, and as long as there have been people living in the northwest part of the state near the Alabama border, there have been stories about this hideous swamp-dwelling monster.

The first accounts came years ago from the mouths of southern workingmen. It wasn't a common thing, but every so often, loggers, hunters or trappers would come into town buzzing over some story about the beast in the swamp. What did this beast look like?

Many weren't able to say. Many people couldn't say to have seen the Skunkape, but had heard it loud and clear—a terrible high-pitched scream that ripped through the night, scaring men near out of their wits. Those who were able to muster enough courage to investigate often spied an enormous shadow loping away into the swamp, leaving a rotten stench in its wake. These were the lucky ones.

Some hunters slogging through swamps in the northern parts of Escambia County spoke of coming face to face with the ugliest thing they had ever seen while venturing through the sloughs. The men who saw it clearly described a creature that caused people to blanch in fear or laugh in disbelief. Covered head to foot in a wretched mass of stinking hair, it was said to stand over eight feet tall, with huge arms that hung down past its knees. The smell emanating from it was bad enough to make a person gag.

Not a pretty picture, but one that seemed to stick. Throughout the 19th century and to the present day, sightings of the aptly named Skunkape continue to circulate. "Ted Macke," a pseudonym for a swamp lover from the southeastern part of the state, relates his own experience with the legendary beast in the swamps of Escambia:

"Swamps have always been my favorite place to go, so I guess I settled in the right state," Macke says. "I make as many trips to the Everglades as I can, and when I've got some extra time off, I try to visit some place I haven't been before. It was back in the summer of '89, and me and Rush—he's my dog—were doing a bit of exploring in the Escambia swamplands around the Perdido River.

"I had heard the story about that damn Skunkape, but if anyone ever came up to me saying they'd seen him, I'd call them crazy. That was until I saw the thing with my own two eyes. Now, I guess I've got different ideas."

It was dusk, and Ted was starting to think about a place to set up camp. "The first sign that something might be lurking was the smell. Rush smelled it before me, and he was going nuts, barking like crazy at the trees," Ted says. "It was unlike him, so I had my eyes peeled, wondering what he was seeing."

Not seeing—smelling. "I'm telling you, the smell almost knocked me out of my boat. It was *bad*. Really, really *bad*. If I had to describe it, I'd say a cross between blue cheese, rotten meat and skunk. It was honestly the worst thing I'd ever smelled." Quite the statement coming from someone who spends so much of his time in swampland, but Macke takes pains to make something clear. "I've smelled some rotten things in swamps before, make no mistake, but this was different. I almost turned my boat around right then and there."

Ignoring his instincts, Macke kept his boat moving forward, not knowing what was coming. "All hell broke loose a second later. We were brushing a bit too close to the bank and there was this crazy crashing around in the trees and brush. Then we heard a huge splash. Something big was emerging, and Rush was losing his mind."

In a moment of cacophonous horror, the Skunkape came crashing through the bush, an impossibly enormous beast with long, hairy, flailing arms, splashing in the water. "I didn't get a clear, unobstructed look at it," Macke says. "It was still in the trees and moving away from us, but I could tell that whatever it was, it was *big*." At the sight of Ted Macke and his dog, the creature raised its head and let out a high-pitched shriek so loud that Macke immediately covered his ears. The smell of rot, which had been bad before, thickened.

"I didn't waste a second turning that boat around and heading back," Macke says. "I had it on full throttle. I did not sleep much at my camp that night and Rush was shaking until the morning, as though he had gotten a look at a long-dead ancestor."

Macke still considers himself a swampland enthusiast, but after his experience on the Alabama border, his interests have been overshadowed by cryptozoology—the study of monsters. "I'd never believed in Bigfoot or Yetis or the Loch Ness monster," he says. "Always made me laugh, really. Thought it was bunk. But after my visit to

Escambia, I couldn't help but think, *Okay. There* are *things out there that we don't know about.*" He's currently planning a trip up to Scotland to catch a glimpse of Loch Ness.

Who knows what Ted Macke really saw in the sloughs of western Florida. Intent on maintaining his privacy, he insists that his real name be kept from these pages, all the while admitting that he "didn't get a clear, unobstructed look at it." Still, he insists on being completely sure of three things: it was big, it was humanoid and it was hairy. Readers may say that such a description fits half of Alabama's backwoodsmen. Could this be a case of a solitary man with an overactive imagination?

The answer will largely depend on readers' inclinations. Have we humans already discovered every major species on earth? Have all forms of life already been slotted away in their appropriate categories—genus, class, phylum? Or are there yet some species that have escaped the human gaze? Maybe we'll know for sure the day all the swamps are drained and replaced by housing developments, or the day the Skunkape is captured and put on display in the Miami Metrozoo. Maybe it would be better if that day never comes.

Mystery of the Kissimmee

With a population of over 17 million, Florida is ranked the fourth most populated state in the United States. No one living in the southeast part of the state should be too surprised by this figure, for it is nothing but concrete, strip malls and continuous settlement all the way up the eastern shore, from Miami to Port St. Lucie. Take into account all the other major population centers—the Tampa/St. Petersburg area, Jacksonville and Orlando—and it becomes all too clear where all the people are: crowded into huge urban areas that keep growing bigger and bigger by the year.

Yet, there is another side to Florida. Even as urban settlements encroach into the swampland and forest, even as the rivers are drained and land is cleared to make way for the ever-increasing number of people, there are still parts of the state that are virtually undisturbed. A huge expanse of the Everglades running west past Miami and through the interior, swamps and forests of the eastern panhandle and the vast tracts of subtropical landscape that make up the central lake lands all remain relatively untouched. Travelers to these parts of the state would be hard pressed to find any similarities to the densely populated urban sprawl where the majority of Floridians reside. Out in the country, it's an entirely different world, with its own pace, its own ways and its own mysteries.

The Kissimmee River flows through the subtropical verdure of central Florida. It is a major waterway that connects Lake Okeechobee and Lake Kissimmee, and it

Dark waters of the Kissimmee

once served as a major route of transportation through the heart of the state. Now that Florida's paved thoroughfares have replaced rivers as the main arteries for transportation, the Kissimmee River flows silently once more, through vast and unpopulated lands.

On most maps, the river is depicted as a crooked blue line, running north to south. It draws the boundary between four counties and spans the length of the Avon Park Air Force Range, linking two major lakes. This solitary blue line is intersected by only three roads, nowhere near anything resembling a major city. It is obvious with one look at any map that the Kissimmee flows through the middle of nowhere.

Most state maps, though, are drawn by people who usually don't bother with too many details of the middle-of-nowhere places. This is blatantly obvious to anyone who has ever taken a canoe down the Kissimmee. Murky waters meander through lush wetlands, fed by innumerable inlets partially concealed by thick vegetation, dotted by unmarked ponds that open up along its length; the Kissimmee is nothing at all like a sterile blue line.

Rick Selzer, a boating enthusiast with a fondness for Florida's wetlands, would certainly be able to attest to this fact. "I've taken more than one boat trip on the Kissimmee," he says. "It's probably one of my favorite trips to make; that's some real great country. There are times when it gets quiet out on that water, and you feel like you could be the only person in the world. Just you and the river—it's something else. It gets you thinking about things. Makes you humble because you realize how small you are in this big world. There is a sort of mystery about it. It has a way of calming you."

Selzer's hardly the first to talk this way about the spectacle of nature undisturbed. And yet, he's quick to add: "But there are other stretches of that river that give you a cold, hard feeling in your gut. Where the bush on either side starts to look dark, dangerous, and you can start to feel darn uneasy about being out there alone. If Mother Nature decided it was time to teach you a thing or two, there wouldn't be a hell of a lot you could do about it."

Though he speaks of "Mother Nature," as Selzer continues it becomes clear that it isn't really nature that he is talking about, or at least not nature as most people understand it. "I'm not a superstitious guy, and I've never really believed in ghosts or any of that, but there are things that have happened on that river that have definitely changed my outlook. I'll just say there is something to the stories about that river. I'll tell you that much."

Stories about the river? There are skeptics, of course. People who have spent a lot of time on the Kissimmee and swear that there is nothing to the tales of the weird goings-on in the bush. Exaggerations and overactive imaginations, the scoffers say, nothing out there but what ought to be. The weird sounds? A wild hog crashing through the broadleaf marsh. The violent splashing? An alligator going after its prey. The ransacked campsites? A rare Florida panther helping itself to unattended food. Whatever bizarre phenomena the superstitious offer, there seem to always be explanations that counter; there is no mystery in the bush, only flora, the fauna and a quiet river.

Rick Selzer may have agreed at one time, but no longer. "For the most part, I didn't think too much of the stories, one way or another," he says. "None of that kind of stuff interested me, and no one I knew personally had ever experienced it. It was one of those 'friend-of-a-friend' things. The stories were always about what had happened to someone else—usually someone's friend or cousin. "

Regardless, Rick Selzer never gave much thought to the tales of the strange things said to go on in the Kissimmee between the Avon Park Air Force Range and the town of Basinger. "The explanations were pretty out there," Selzer says. "Sometimes you heard that there were the ghosts of pirates who, hundreds of years ago, had fought to the death over—you guessed it—buried treasure. There were the other stories about some poor guy getting it from some alligator a while ago, and that his spirit was still in the waters, making a big racket come nighttime.

"I don't know what to make of any of that," Selzer continues, "but I'll say this much. There's no way that whatever is going on out there is natural. No fish, reptile or animal could have been responsible for the things I saw."

It began as a trip like any other. Rick Selzer, alone, piloting his boat down the Kissimmee, enjoying the silence and the solitude of the wilderness. "I was about half an hour past the Air Force Range, the sun was getting low and I was thinking about finding a good patch of ground to set up camp when I heard the splash."

"I didn't think anything of it," Selzer continues. "Just curious, as always, and I usually make a habit of investigating whenever I hear something. So, I steered to where I heard the splash—had my eyes peeled, thinking along the lines of a gator or a jumping fish or maybe a hunting heron."

The sound had come from a small bay off the side of the river that was partly concealed by dense overhanging flora. "The second time I heard the splashing it was much louder," Selzer says. "It got me going, that second time. I sped up a bit because I didn't want to miss it." Making his way through the narrow inlet, Selzer found himself in a bay he'd never seen before: a small body of still water hedged in on all sides by thick marsh and heavy tree growth. Selzer piloted his boat into the bay, took one look around and instantly had an uneasy feeling.

"Right away, it felt like there was something wrong," he says. "No, wait. I should say it felt like *everything* was wrong. It was the water, the bush, everything. The sun was just starting to go down, and it was starting to get dark, but wasn't nearly dark enough to explain the color of the water. This water, it was *black*—way too black to be natural. I remember looking at it and thinking, *what is going on?* And then when I saw the brush, I just wanted to get of there."

Selzer's description borders on the surreal: twisting branches reaching out over the water like claws, dark and dense willows that seemed to be hiding a million hostile shadows. Suddenly, Selzer felt extremely cold and forgot all about the splashing that had lured him closer. He began turning his vessel around. "I admit it. I chickened out. Whatever was going on, I didn't want anything to do with it."

Then the splashing started up again. But this time it wasn't so much splashing as it was a huge watery upheaval. The center of the pond rose up with a tremendous force and fell back on itself with a massive splash, followed by a violent churning, like something huge was thrashing just under the surface. "My heart must have been going a million beats a minute," says Selzer, "and I was backing up as fast as my boat could go, but I still couldn't help myself. I stopped for a second to take a look."

He was convinced that what he was seeing wasn't natural. "Nothing that lives in the wetlands is big enough to make that kind of stir," he says. "But beyond its size, I could tell that there was nothing there—there was nothing under the surface. The water was churning on its own, as if the whole bay was alive." Alive and apparently unhappy that he was there.

"I was back on the Kissimmee pretty quick after that, going full throttle downriver and not even thinking about looking back. I kept going until I found a safe place to set up camp." But Selzer wasn't out of the woods just yet; for whatever reason, the spirits of the Kissimmee River seemed set on tormenting him.

"Falling asleep that night was tough," Selzer says. "I don't know how long I was tossing around, wondering at every sound. I'd never felt so out of place in this natural setting. My mind started playing weird games. I started to think that the river was alive, flowing with evil intentions. I don't know why, but it was like the Kissimmee didn't want me around that day."

With troubled thoughts, Selzer fell into a fitful sleep. "I don't know how long I was out for," Selzer says. "It couldn't have been long. I woke up with my eyes burning and my head running circles. I wasn't up for more than a few seconds before I knew things were wrong. Something had woken me, and the hair on the back of my neck stood erect when that feeling I had in the bay earlier that night returned. I couldn't see a thing, but I was sure that whatever was out there was watching me."

His hunch was confirmed when he heard a spine-tingling moan from the darkness. High-pitched and terrible, sounding as though it could have just as easily been beast as man, the wail was coming from the direction of the river. "I jumped out of my sleeping bag right away," Selzer says. "The thing was so loud, it couldn't have been more than 30 feet away. I had my flashlight and my knife out. Looking back, I don't know what I was thinking. Actually, I still don't know what to think."

When the howl sounded again, Selzer acted. "I remember thinking that maybe this thing is some kind of animal, and dogs came to mind. Chase a dog, and nine times out of ten, that dog will run. Run from a dog, and it will come after you." So what did Selzer do?

"I ran out to the river, knife in one hand, flashlight in the other, more buzzed than scared. My blood was rushing, but I was more eager to see what this creature looked like than fearful."

But when he reached the bank of the Kissimmee, he found nothing. Standing breathless, he scanned the surrounding bushes and waters with his flashlight, still eager for a sighting of whatever he'd heard howling. Minutes passed, and still there was nothing. Only silence. "I was a bit disappointed, that's for sure," Selzer continues. "Part of me wanted to believe that I was going to see an animal that no one had ever seen before. It's a natural reaction, I think—curiosity." But curiosity was not all that he was feeling. The silence of the Kissimmee wetlands that Rick had always enjoyed suddenly took on an oppressive weight. Where had this creature disappeared to? "I was standing there, and the more I thought about it, the more apprehensive I became. Where had it gone? Why hadn't I heard anything? If it had run into the bush, I definitely would have heard a rustling, or a splash if it had gone into the water. The quiet really started to bug me. For a second I started to wonder if maybe the sound had been a dream or something. Maybe everything that had happened had been a dream. Maybe I was going crazy."

Rick made his way back to his campsite, thinking through the events of the last several hours, trying to

come up with some sort of rational explanation for all
that had happened that day. But that was before he
reached the small clearing where he was camped. What he
found there dashed all hopes of any kind of rational
explanation.

"My campsite looked like a hurricane had passed
through it. My tent was collapsed, my sleeping bag was
inside out, and draped over a bush, all my bags were
emptied, my gear scattered all over the place." Selzer knew
that he hadn't heard anything ransacking his campsite,
and logic told him that this kind of mess would have
involved a huge noise. His first thought was that a wild
animal had gone through his things.

"Impossible as it seemed, it was the only explanation
I allowed for," Selzer says. "It was the only thing that made
sense to me. Problem was, when I turned on my lantern
and started cleaning up, dawned on me that there was no
way any animal did this. First of all, even though my food
was scattered all over the place, none of it was touched or
missing. Not so much as a bite from any of it."

But when Selzer noticed that there wasn't a single animal track in his campsite—not so much as a solitary paw
or claw imprint in the dirt—that his thoughts turned to
the tales he'd heard about the Kissimmee. "One of the
things that you hear about is how people's campsites are
ransacked at night. Up until then, I would have just thought
that animals got loose in their food. But when I was putting all my stuff back together, I knew there was no way
this was an animal. Something else had been on my site,
and it wasn't anything that anyone has ever shot or eaten
or put in a zoo."

Without another wink of sleep for the rest of the night, Selzer got back on the river at first light and wasted no time heading back to his truck. He drove off swearing to himself that he'd never take another trip on the Kissimmee. "That was a few years ago," Rick says with a laugh, "but I've always been terrible at keeping promises, and it was only a matter of time before I broke that one."

Having recently returned from another trip on the Kissimmee, Rick says that as anxious as he was at the outset, it wasn't long before the peace and quiet of the river and the surrounding wetland brought him a familiar solace. "It's funny how you can get used to the idea of almost anything. There was a time after that trip when those strange events were all I could think about. Had it been the ghosts of dead pirates, or the ghost of a guy taken by alligators? Hell…UFOs? Maybe it was some animal after all, and I missed the tracks. It was dark, I was rattled—can't say. I don't know anymore."

And nothing was clarified during his most recent trip. "Nothing happened my last time out and that's the way I like it," Selzer says. "Just me, the river and my own thoughts." That said, during his last excursion, the river enthusiast did make a point of staying clear of any concealed bays, and when he camped, he kept all his gear sealed and tied down. "Never know," he laughs. "Maybe the only thing that kept them ghost pirates from taking all my stuff last time was no pockets to put it all in. Trust me, I won't be taking chances with them again."

4

Haunted Businesses

The Don CeSar

A woman crosses the opulent lobby of the Don CeSar hotel. Outside, a swollen Florida sun is dipping towards the horizon, and the first traces of a pink and purple sunset splash across the gulf waters. Golden light filters onto the hotel's main floor, where the woman is waiting by the elevator. Having spent most of the day lying idly on a towel underneath the sun, she feels relaxed, sleepy even, and isn't too mindful of her surroundings; her attention is partly taken by the elevator door in front of her, but mostly by the feeling of her pleasant afterglow.

The door opens and the woman steps inside. She's instantly conscious of a coolness, like air conditioning set a bit too high, but she doesn't give it much thought. It actually feels nice against the heat of the late afternoon. She moves to the panel on the wall for the controls, and is slightly surprised to see that the button for her floor is already lit. The elevator lurches to life, and she realizes she isn't alone.

"Enjoying your time here?" The voice is friendly, calm, but the woman still starts. She could have sworn there was no one in the elevator when she walked in. She looks toward the voice; there's a pleasant-looking, middle-aged man with silver hair standing in the corner, his fine suit and easy confidence lending him an aristocratic air. The man smiles, and she relaxes.

"Yes," she says, taking off her sunglasses and smiling back. "It was a gorgeous day, just gorgeous, and I had nothing to do but lie around and enjoy it."

"I'm glad to hear it," the man replies. "It's easy to keep our guests happy when the weather cooperates the way it has been."

So, the woman realizes, *he must manage the resort.* "Good for business," she says.

"If you want to put it that way," the man shrugs. "And I suppose I'm fortunate to be banking on sunshine in a part of the world that has so much of it."

"If only I could find a way to make a profit off the rain in Seattle," she says with a laugh.

The man smiles, and then leans forward, his voice dropping slightly. "I'll let you in on something," he says, his expression suddenly serious. "Not everyone knows this, but the Don CeSar isn't just about money." He glances around him, at the walls, the roof, appraising the small space of the elevator as though the walls can hear him. "No. Profit is not what has made this resort great."

Something about the man's manner has drawn the woman in. She finds herself following his gaze, to the walls and roof. "No?" she whispers, following his sudden discretion.

"No," the man responds. "Love is what made this place—a man's love for a woman. All the money in the world won't change that fact."

The elevator stops, and the man's serious expression melts back into a disarming smile. "But these are only details, I suppose. What matters most is that the sun is shining and that you're enjoying your time here with us."

The woman smiles back. She says, "Thanks, sir. *That* I am." And though she wonders whose love it was, exactly, that made the Don CeSar, she finds herself walking toward the open door. *Another time,* she thinks. *I'll likely see the man sometime later in the week. I'll ask him about the story of the Don CeSar then.*

Stepping out of the elevator, she turns. "Well, I've got to get ready for dinner, but you'll have to tell me all about the…" she stops mid-sentence, hissing a sharp intake of breath. There's no one in the elevator. It's empty. The man she'd just been speaking to is nowhere to be seen.

So goes another sighting of the venerable ghost of the Don CeSar Hotel in St. Petersburg, possibly the most romantic haunt in the state of Florida, if not the country. The woman could have been any one of the thousands of visitors that fly down to the five star resort every winter. For years now, the ghost of Thomas Rowe has been making rounds of the hotel he opened so many years ago, pulling back chairs, opening doors, checking to make sure his guests are enjoying themselves. And sometimes, just sometimes, giving them a little backstory about the state's historic vacation spot. It wasn't for the money, you understand. Thomas Rowe did it all for love…

Her name was Lucinda, a young Spanish opera singer with a striking face and coal black hair whose success on the stages across Europe was just beginning. It was the late 1890s, and Thomas Rowe was just a lowly American student studying abroad in London, England. But the moment the talented singer met Thomas' gaze, their fate was locked.

A passionate affair followed. Rowe had taken to calling Lucinda "Maritana," the name of the gypsy heroine in the opera she was starring in. And she, in turn, called her lover Don CeSar, after the hero of her operatic hit.

Although Maritana and Don CeSar enjoyed a happily-ever-after on stage, Thomas and Lucinda's story would not be so auspicious. As is so often the case with thwarted young love, it amounted to parental disapproval.

Lucinda was young and gifted. A lifetime of musical training was just beginning to pay off, and her parents weren't about to sit back and let a love affair jeopardize everything she had worked so hard for. "Who is this man, Thomas Rowe?" they asked. A nobody, that's who. A green youth, with no wealth or pedigree. An American who didn't even share the same religion. It was impossible. Lucinda's family would not allow the union.

For a short while, Thomas and Lucinda persisted, meeting in secret by an ornate fountain in the streets of London, exchanging passionate promises, declaring their love for each other, carrying on the way all star-crossed lovers are wont to do. In the end, Lucinda's parents remained firm—there was no way they would allow the pair to be together. They made it clear that choosing Thomas was choosing to leave the family, and as far as Lucinda was concerned, she had no choice. The couple met by their fountain for the last time on a cold and foggy London night, where a tearful Lucinda told her Don CeSar that she wouldn't be able to see him anymore. Thomas, always a gentleman, saw that Lucinda had made up her mind, and any argument on his part would just make their parting more difficult.

And so the brokenhearted Thomas Rowe turned his back on his Spanish paramour and returned to the United States. There, he immersed himself in business, quickly becoming a millionaire through Florida real estate. As busy as Thomas became, however, he never forgot Lucinda. For two years, he wrote her regularly, even though all of his letters came back unopened. He'd gotten so used to seeing his letters come back from London that he had no idea what to do with himself the day an envelope scrawled with Lucinda's writing fell on his desk.

He opened it, and Lucinda broke Thomas Rowe's heart for the second time. According to legend, the letter read:

Tom, my beloved Don CeSar,

> *This life is only an intermediate plane. I leave it without regret and travel to a place where the swing of the pendulum does not bring pain. Time is infinite. I wait for you by our fountain to share our timeless love forever.*

By the time he'd gotten the letter, Lucinda was dead.

Thomas buried the loss deep inside, learning to live with it as the months turned to years, which turned to decades. It wasn't until 1924, when he moved to St. Petersburg, that the now-prosperous businessman began dreaming of constructing the monument that he would dedicate to his love.

The Don CeSar Hotel took three years to build. Completed in 1928 with a $1.2 million price tag, the hotel was 300 percent over budget. But this didn't seem to matter to Rowe. The towering structure overlooking St. Pete's beach belonged as much to him as it did to the Spanish opera singer he'd never stopped loving. In honor of Lucinda's heritage, Thomas had it built with a distinct

Spanish style, complete with Moorish towers and high arched windows. In the center of the courtyard was an extravagant fountain that was said to be a replica of the one in London that had been their meeting place so many years ago.

While Thomas was alive, the Don CeSar prospered. Considered one of Florida's most luxurious resorts, it drew no shortage of celebrated guests. From F. Scott Fitzgerald to Teddy Roosevelt to Al Capone, America's rich and famous came to St. Petersburg to spend time under the Florida sun and enjoy the luxuries of Rowe's hotel. The hotel prospered, and Thomas Rowe became very wealthy.

But it was obvious to anyone who knew Rowe that money was not his primary motivation. No. It wasn't the money, but the hotel, that he was enamored with. This was obvious to anyone who'd seen him walking through the grand lobby, chatting with guests, exuding an unmistakable aura of peace and contentment. He would welcome people into the Don CeSar with warmth and enthusiasm, as if he was welcoming them into his home. There were other times, during especially striking sunsets, when Rowe could be found by the big fountain in the courtyard, staring at the waters with a happy smile, as though the running waters were whispering blessings only he could hear. For 12 years, Rowe rarely strayed far from the Don CeSar, living on the fifth floor and managing many of the daily affairs of the elegant hotel overlooking the Gulf of Mexico.

Rowe's integral role in the Don CeSar's success became unmistakeably clear after 1940, the year he collapsed while making his rounds through the lobby. Refusing to be taken to the hospital, he was moved upstairs to his room, where nurses and medical equipment were brought up to take care of him during his final days. Before he died, Rowe made it clear to his lawyer that he wished to leave the Don CeSar to the hotel staff. After years of training his staff to treat his beloved hotel as if it was their own, he was confident there was no one else better qualified to run the building in his absence. Yet according to legend, the nurses tending to Rowe refused to sign the will as witnesses, claiming that their patient was in no shape to sign away such an enormous property. He would never get another chance to bequeath the hotel to the Don CeSar staff. Falling unconscious shortly after being moved to his bedroom, Thomas Rowe died soon after. His estranged wife, Mary Rowe, was given the deed to the hotel instead.

The Don CeSar's fortunes rapidly plummeted. The country was hurled into the Second World War in December 1941 when Pearl Harbor was bombed, and everyone seemed to lose their desire for vacationing; almost all reservations were cancelled. Mary Rowe ended up selling the hotel to the military in 1942, and for the rest of the war, it served as a convalescence center for wounded airmen. By the 1960s, the Don CeSar was almost unrecognizable. Over two decades of military ownership had transformed it from a luxury resort into office space. Its opulence traded in for functionality, the hotel no longer had a courtyard; Rowe's beloved fountain had been demolished and the rest of the hotel seemed destined to go the way of the fountain.

Abandoned and in terrible disrepair by 1969, the Don CeSar was slated for demolition. Oddly enough, Rowe's preference for architectural grandeur was what saved it from being relegated to rubble. The enormous hotel would cost too much to demolish, and so was saved from the wrecking ball in time for a group of local preservationists to gather resources to save the now-historic building. Renovations began in the early 1970s, the first in a long series of huge cash investments which led to the fully restored and thriving five star resort that stands today. It might be said that the Don CeSar was resurrected from the dead. And if there is any truth to the numerous goings-on reported soon after renovations began, the hotel wasn't the only thing that was resurrected.

Rowe began appearing in the 1970s to the first wave of renovators. A thin man with silver hair and a tailored suit, looking decidedly out of place among the sweating workers, he never got in the way or said a word to anyone, but watched them carefully as they went about their work. Because of his air of authority and the frequent attention he gave to their progress, the renovators assumed he was an owner or manager. When the workers got around to asking management what the quiet man in the gray hair was doing on the work site, they discovered that he wasn't a part of the new owner's team; no one knew who this man was.

He continued to appear to guests and employees after the renovations were complete and the hotel was reopened. His lobby seemed to be his favorite place; with his calm smile and dignified bearing, he engaged guests in conversation, welcoming them to the Don CeSar, urging them to inform the staff if there was anything that could make their stay more enjoyable.

Something about the man always seemed out of place. The suit he wore was too old-fashioned to be so immaculately pressed and fitted. His manner was overly formal for the time, his speech anachronistic. It was obvious to anyone who was approached by him that there was something odd about the kind man. But it wasn't long before the reason for his oddities was discovered. The man was Thomas Rowe, and Thomas Rowe, as we know, is dead.

It isn't known who identified the mysterious man in the hotel as the former owner. A Don CeSar employee who had seen photographs of Rowe? A guest who knew the history of the building? Or perhaps an older guest who had known Rowe when he was still alive? No one knows for sure, but once it was suggested, word spread quickly about the ghost of the Don CeSar's former proprietor.

Certainly, death had changed none of his habits. He still loved to walk among the hotel guests, eager to ensure that all who visited were enjoying the place as much as he did. During especially impressive sunsets, he was also spotted in the courtyard or out on St. Pete's beach, watching the blazing colors close the day. He was also known to engage lone guests in conversation in the elevators, and had a tendency to walk the halls of the fifth floor. When he did appear, he rarely stuck around for more than several minutes. Sometimes he would vanish into thin air, as quickly as he had appeared; other times, he would simply walk into a crowd in the lobby and disappear among the bodies.

No one knew what to make of the reappearance of Thomas Rowe, especially the Don CeSar management.

On one hand, the dead owner's spirit was not doing anything inappropriate. None of the guests had complained about their encounters with him; in fact, he seemed to cast a favorable impression on those he spoke with. On the other hand, the management was not eager to advertise that a dead man walked the halls of their resort. Although most of the employees didn't mind the presence of the former owner, some of the managers—especially those who had run-ins with him—were a bit unsettled by Rowe. What did he want? Was it a mere love for his hotel that kept him around? Why did those who saw him in the courtyard or on the beach walk away with the impression that he was *waiting* for something? What could the dead man possibly be waiting for? The eventual appearance of another mysterious figure may have provided an answer to these questions.

She began appearing in the 1980s. Clothed in an enormous dress that looked like it may have been lifted from the set of *Gone With the Wind,* she was a striking woman with black hair and dramatic features. Only ever seen in the courtyard or on the beach, and only during sunset, she always appeared standing next to the silver-haired spirit.

They don't say a word to each other as the sun dips below the gulf. What happens next depends on who is telling the story. Sometimes, the couple slowly disappears with the fading light. In other reports, they walk down the beach, hand in hand, before vanishing into dusk's darkness.

Whatever the case, it seems that since the 80s, Thomas Rowe has been entertaining a rather special guest at the Don CeSar. And of course, those familiar with his story have not hesitated in identifying the woman with the big dress and black hair. Has the owner of the grand hotel on St. Pete's beach finally been reunited with his beloved Spanish opera singer? There have been fewer and fewer sightings of Thomas Rowe in the lobby and elevators and on the fifth floor since the woman began to appear by his side. Indeed, it seems that the arrival of the woman who inspired the Don CeSar has led Rowe to neglect his duties. Given the overwhelming amount of overtime the old businessman has put into the building, it would be hard to fault him for taking time off. He definitely deserves it. Now the question is, how long will Lucinda remain at the Don CeSar, and when she departs, will Thomas go with her? Only time will tell.

Presidents, Gangsters and Ghosts

Imagine a guest staying at one of the must luxurious hotels in the country. Is this guest a man? A woman? Is this guest young? Old? On holidays, or in town on business? It doesn't matter, whatever image works best, just imagine a guest at one of the most luxurious hotels in the country. Now imagine what this guest would think if, upon waking up one morning, he or she looked across their room, to see a man, a complete stranger, standing in hospital pyjamas and robe. How would this guest react? Startled, confused, angry? Now imagine, after a few seconds, the stranger vanishes into thin air, just like that— poof!—gone. What would this guest think now? What would this guest do? For readers who have stayed at the Biltmore Hotel in Corral Gables, Miami, the above scenario might not require much imagination. Indeed, there is a chance that such readers recall such an experience.

One thing that is common knowledge among anyone familiar with ghost stories is that haunted places are usually imbued with tumultuous or, at the very least, unusual histories. Ghosts are rarely the product of humdrum circumstances, so it ought not be too surprising that the Biltmore Hotel is said to be full of them.

The story of the Biltmore begins harmlessly enough, with two rich men named George Merrick and John McEntee, and their dream of building the grandest hotel in the United States, if not the world. Although a dream of this magnitude would be considered ambitious by any-one's standards, in the 1920s, such a vision meant some-thing else all together. For if the old adage "they don't build them like they used to" can be applied to anything at all, it would definitely sum up the construction of luxury hotels at that time.

Historically speaking, the 1920s mark the tail end of what is known as the Gilded Age, a period between the Civil War and the Great Depression when the rich became grossly rich, and huge numbers of the not-so-rich were put to work making the grossly rich even richer. It was before the rise of what we now call mass consumerism, where the idea of luxury was reserved for a very small number of gilded Americans, and the luxuries this privi-leged class enjoyed made so much of what we call luxury today seem dismally proletarian in comparison.

Merrick and McEntee's Biltmore Hotel, located in the affluent neighborhood of Coral Gables, would stand as one of the best examples of Gilded Age luxury. Featuring an enormous colonnaded lobby with a barrel-vaulted ceiling, Oriental carpets thrown over travertine floors, marble-furnished rooms and sprawling pools, the Biltmore was constructed with royalty in mind, and when it was opened to the public in January 1926, royalty came to visit. There was royalty of all stripes: Old World royalty represented by the likes of the Duke and Duchess of Windsor, Democratic royalty like Bing Crosby, Judy Garland and the Roosevelts and, most famously, the undisputed Czar of the Underworld, Al Capone.

There are no noteworthy stories regarding Capone's visits to the Biltmore, so we can only assume that the king

The Biltmore Hotel, Coral Gables, Miami

of organized crime was well behaved. The same cannot be said, however, of two lesser thugs, Arthur Clark and Thomas "Fatty" Walsh. A pair of New York mobsters who fled south to evade police, Clark and Walsh arrived at the Biltmore in 1928, and they promptly went about setting up shop.

In this case, "shop" was an illegal gambling house and speakeasy on the hotel's 13th and 14th floors that catered to Miami's rich and famous. The illegal sale of alcohol was a lucrative business during the prohibition period, and Clark and Walsh made a killing off their black-tie enterprise. Unfortunately for Fatty Walsh, this killing eventually led to his murder, when less than one year later, in March 1929, his partner shot him to death in the middle of the gambling floor after a heated argument. The room had been full of witnesses when Fatty was shot, but by the time the police arrived the only thing left was Walsh's bleeding body. No witnesses, no tables, no bar, no booze. The crime went unpunished.

But not unforgotten. Throughout the following decade, as the hotel weathered on through the hard times of the Depression, strange stories began to circulate about the 13th floor. Guests and employees alike spoke of hearing faint whispers and chuckles when there was no one else in the room, a faint apparition that sometimes appeared in mirror's reflections and elevators that would stop on the 13th floor, whether or not number 13 had been pressed.

Just when the Biltmore was acquiring a reputation for its resident ghostly gangster, however, the Second World War broke out. Like so many other vacation resorts across

the country, the Biltmore suffered major financial problems at the outset of the war, and when the United States
officially entered the war in December 1941, the hotel was
purchased by the government and converted to a hospital
by the War Department. The ensuing years brought a sad
rush of new "guests" to the hotel-turned-hospital. There
was probably very little the ghost of a prohibitionist era
gangster could do to rattle men wounded in the fires of
the Second World War, and if Fatty Walsh was still up to
his supernatural highjinks, no one seemed to notice. As its
brilliant travertine floors were covered with linoleum, its
windows boarded up and covered with concrete, the
hotel, along with its resident ghost, was largely forgotten
over the war years. All its finery was gone—its vain glit-
terati replaced by wounded soldiers.

It remained a medical facility after the war, housing the
University of Miami's School of Medicine for a short
time, only to be shut down and abandoned in 1973. The
City of Coral Gables took possession of the hotel then,
and for the next 10 years, it stood vacant. Or that was the
official story, anyway.

Yet those who found themselves in the vicinity of the
old hotel at night often had good reason to doubt the
official story. If there was truly no one in the big old
building, how could the lights be explained? Over 30 years
after the last guest had cautiously related an experience
with the ghost of Fatty Walsh, people began to talk once
more about the spirits at Biltmore again. And it all started
because of the lights.

What lights? The lights that danced in the former
hotel windows after the sun went down. The lights that

intermittently flashed, and were visible from almost any point on the surrounding 18-hole golf course. For a while, the lights in the windows became a bit of an attraction among Coral Gable youngsters, many of whom went out at night to sit and take in the show.

Word of weird goings-on at Biltmore began to spread once more. In 1978, a group of supernatural enthusiasts managed to secure permission to investigate the site. Together with a team of psychics, the group ventured into the hotel intending to conduct a séance and perhaps come up with some explanations for the strange phenomena occurring in the building. By all accounts, it turned out to be quite the evening.

First, without any knowledge of the building's past, the psychics were let loose in the building. It was instantly obvious to all of them that the place was haunted. They all spoke of myriad energies and vibrations all over the hotel. Some spoke of negative energies, of vibrations that emanated fear and pain. There were a number of floors that had more than a few spirits trapped within their psychic prisons. Others sensed solitary spirits content to wander, and some spirits that were actually merry; most of the psychics claimed that there was some major paranormal energy in all the elevators. But almost all of them eventually zeroed in on the 13th and 14th floors.

That was where they conducted their séance and clued in to several telling premonitions. They picked up on a lot of competing energies: excitement, pleasure, loss. There was laughter in these rooms, they said, a lot of laughter; perhaps hundreds of spirits were there, contributing to a cacophony of something that resembled mindless happiness. But there was also tragedy. Near the fireplace on the 13th floor, there was fear and a killing. A strong presence was still there. This presence wasn't pained, angry or dangerous, but was hanging around. It felt it belonged there. Or rather, *he* belonged. A number of the sensitives insisted that they were dealing with a man.

Later, when the psychics were listening to an audio recording of their séance, they heard a mysterious noise that no one had noticed while the séance was underway. The sound began as a gentle tapping and continued to get louder until it had become a rhythmic pounding, threatening to drown out the voices of those participating in the séance. No one in the room had heard the sound at the time it was recorded.

Encouraged by these findings, another group of paranormal investigators ventured into the hotel one year later, in 1979. Unlike the psychics who went before, these individuals entered the building with hardware in lieu of psychic talents. Equipped with their cameras, tape recorders and thermometers, they made their way through the building taking measurements, making observations, and recording all of the proceedings on audio tape. Unlike the psychics, these investigators were familiar with the hotel's history, and though they would have been excited at the psychics' affirmations of the building's phenomena, there was some skepticism.

They were surprised, however, when they played back their tape recordings. Among the paranormal snoop's most valued tools, the tape recorder is used extensively by every investigator who takes the pastime seriously. For those unfamiliar with the practice, the tape recorder is used to measure EVP (electronic voice phenomenon) that may occur during an investigation. If ever there were a bible written for paranormal investigation, it would state as one of its main tenets that, although the naked ear rarely detects anything out of the ordinary in the course of a ghost hunt, a running tape recorder will pick up all sorts of inexplicable noises.

After the investigators at the Biltmore finished a tranquil tour of the former hotel, they feared that they might not have captured anything at all. After all, they'd ended up tramping around in the building the entire night without so much as a cold spot to show for it. The space seemed dead, inert, and the only noises they expected to hear on their tape recorders was the shuffle of their movement and the sound of their voices. Well, they were wrong. Much to their surprise, a heavy breathing sound registered on a number of their recorders, all on the 13th floor. The breathing was the same on all the tapes—heavy and labored for just over a minute, and ending on a protracted sigh. So, two for two of the paranormal investigations of the old Biltmore Hotel had produced results. Any other group hoping to conduct a third, however, would be disappointed.

In 1983, a city-financed renovation of the old hotel began. The concrete covered windows were reopened and the linoleum was stripped off the travertine floors. Four years later, the hotel opened to the public once more. In 1992, it was purchased by a private consortium, which, over the next 10 years, would invest a staggering $40 million more into renovations. Today, it can safely be said that, in terms of extravagance, the Biltmore Hotel is back to its original standards, receiving guests such as Margaret Thatcher, Bill Clinton and Robert Redford.

Multimillionaires strutting around on a multimillion-dollar stage—as impressive as it may be to many of the Biltmore's guests, the ghosts of the old building seem to be wholly indifferent to it. The good-humored spirit of Fatty Walsh is still said to wander the 13th floor, startling guests and employees alike with friendly chuckles that seem to come out of nowhere, or leaving a scrawling *"Boo!"* on steam-covered bathroom mirrors. He enjoys the elevators, as well, often opening the doors for astonished bellhops and frequently making sure that elevator passengers stop at Floor 13, whether they want to or not. Apparitions of men in hospital garments have been seen on other floors. Seen in suites and hallways, these timid spirits have never interacted with anyone, and they almost always vanish moments after they are spotted.

And so the spirits of the past rub shoulders with the living in the halls of one the country's most luxurious hotels. As far as sites for dead people to haunt, there are certainly far worse places a ghost could be. It may cause one to wonder: are the ghosts of Biltmore aware of their extravagant surroundings? If so, they can hardly be blamed for lingering on.

The St. Francis Inn

On his first night at the St. Francis Inn, the man was woken in the middle of the night by the sound of a woman moaning. His first thought was that the sound was a remnant of a dream. He let a moment pass, blinked once, twice, shook his head and looked up at the darkened ceiling. No. The woman, whoever it was, was still moaning. It wasn't a dream.

He sat up in bed and looked around, trying to figure out where the sound was coming from. It was too close to be coming from another room. He glanced over at the big windows that led out to the balcony. Could there be someone in the courtyard below? That wasn't possible, either. The sound was too clear, so close the woman could have been right next to him. "What the hell is going on?" he muttered aloud, then got out of bed, walked to the bathroom and looked inside. No one there.

Then it got louder, and he started to feel uneasy. Not that he felt threatened; there was nothing about the moan that suggested anything menacing, but it was obvious that the sound could be coming from nowhere else. By the sound of things, some woman was moaning right there in his room, but this simply couldn't be. He was the only person in the room. He paced around for a few more minutes. Looked under the bed, behind the curtains, once more into the courtyard. He flicked on the lights. That didn't help either. If anything it just got louder.

I'm not crazy, the man thought to himself.

"Hello?" he said into the empty room. "Is there anyone there?" That was all it took; the moment the words left his mouth, it stopped, just like that. The sudden silence was almost as disturbing as the moaning had been. Whoever had been making the noise had responded—of this, he was certain. But where was she? Who was she?

This was the man's first night at the inn. Every night after that was more and more strange. On his second night, he was awakened by the television, rapidly switching on and off by itself. Alarmed, he jumped out of bed and went to shut it off, but it wouldn't respond to the control. Only after he shouted at whatever was in his room to stop did the television stop its manic flickering.

His breaking point came after two more nights, when a black woman strode into the middle of his room and started cleaning his bathroom, only to vanish the instant he demanded to know what she was doing. The next morning, he carried his hastily packed bags to the front desk and asked to be moved to another room.

The receptionist didn't need to ask him why. This had happened before—many, many times before. For as long as anyone can remember, visitors staying in Room 3-A at the St. Francis Inn have been having all sorts of bizarre experiences. Management has come to expect guests staying in the room to come downstairs in the morning with some story of what occurred the night before. The fact is that 3-A is Lily's room, and every paranormal enthusiast in the city of St. Augustine knows the tragic story of Lily, the soldier who fell in love with her and the haunted legacy they left behind at the St. Francis Inn.

Located in the heart of St. Augustine's impressive historic district, the St. Francis Inn dates back to 1791, when it was built by a colonist who was granted the land by the Spanish Crown, which ruled the region at the time. It passed through several hands, eventually ending up under the ownership of Colonel Thomas Henry Dummett in 1835. It was at this time that a slave only known by her first name, Lily, was put into service at the Dummett household.

According to the legend, there was a southern gentleman who knew he was in deep trouble the moment he set eyes on Lily. It was another one of those doomed love-at-first-sight scenarios, and the pair proceeded with an affair that was characterized by the two traits necessary for any tragic affair—extraordinarily passionate and explicitly forbidden. The passion was taken care of by the two lovers, but the racial issues of the time forbade their relationship. It was antebellum Florida, after all, and a union between a white man and a black woman could never hope to receive public sanction.

If the man had never given any thought to this social convention before, he became incredibly distraught by it after he fell in love with Lily. They took to meeting in secret in one of the rooms on the third floor of Colonel Dummett's home, and though they were able to steal these moments often enough, they weren't enough for the young man. Apparently not a man used to skulking about, he was ashamed of the secret he was carrying. The fact that he had to sneak about to be with the woman he loved ate him up, and every clandestine meeting with his one-and-only got harder and harder to accept. Then, when word got out about his secret affair, it became unbearable.

Did Lily know how bad it was for her paramour? Impossible to say. But it must have taken her somewhat by surprise when, after their last ardent exchange, her lover bade her a fond farewell and then threw himself out the third story window, dying instantly in the courtyard below, and inevitably ending their affair. Lily, however, would live on. The legend does not recount what happened to her in the following years, but it is likely that she saw the end of the Civil War and emancipation from slavery. Whether she was loved by another, got married or had children is anybody's guess.

Yet, wherever her life took her, she apparently never forgot the man who had thrown himself out a window for her sake. Or that is the assumption, at least—for a long time now, strange things have been afoot on the third floor of the old St. Augustine home. Stories began circulating as early as 1925, when the historic building was converted into a guesthouse. It became the St. Francis Inn in 1948, but no matter what the building has been named, and whoever the owners are, the permanent residents in the room on the third floor seem intent on sticking around.

From the beginning, there hasn't been much doubt about who these residents are. One of the most common sightings has been of an attractive black woman dressed in white, who seems to choose the oddest hours to clean the room. Suddenly appearing in 3-A, often in the middle of the night, she usually heads straight to the bathroom, where she gets down on her knees and scrubs the bathtub.

Those who get out of bed to ask her what she is doing have never have much luck with an answer. Completely ignoring anything asked of her, she scrubs in silence, not even looking up at her startled inquisitors. Ignoring her doesn't work either. Many shocked guests, unsure of what to do, have lain in bed all night, listening to the scrubbing sounds in the next room. What this woman does respond to, however, are orders. Anyone who commands her to stop will see her vanish into thin air. Not for good, though; sometimes she even returns later the same night.

Sometimes she comes to clean; other times, she seems to be engaged in activities that we might only guess at. Some are woken by the sound of a woman moaning, others by the lights in the room strobing on and off. It isn't unknown for the television set to acquire a life of its own, flicking on and off by itself, not responding to its controls. Yet to blame this woman for all of these disturbances might not be completely fair, as she is not the only apparition that is regularly spotted in 3-A.

A man has also been spotted more than once. He is a tall white man dressed in a white shirt, suspenders, long pants and boots. He also appears in the middle of the night, though is never as busy as his fellow phantom in the bathroom. When he does appear, the man's behavior suggests that he is the one responsible for the tinkering with the TV. When he struts into the room, the first thing he does is turn on the television before throwing himself down on a chair in front of it. He isn't a complete couch potato, though. For while people have been woken by the sound of a woman moaning, a man's whispering voice has been heard as well. The whispers are never clear enough to make out clearly, but they are always loud enough to get alarmed guests out of bed and to the light switch.

And is it the man or the woman who has such a fascination with guests' purses, rifling through them at night and leaving them lying on the floor, upturned, their contents scattered? Until someone figures out how to communicate with these two, the question may have to remain unanswered. As for their identities—need it even be clarified? No one doubts that the pair is none other than Lily and her lover. Though it seems, based on all the television watching and bathtub scrubbing, that the years have taken some of the fire out of their affair.

The Tampa Theatre

It is safe to say that most patrons of the old Tampa Bay Theatre have never heard of the ghost of Foster Fink Finley. Among those who have, there are probably few who give the story of the theater's former projectionist much thought. Considering the kind of place the Tampa Theatre has become today, this makes a certain amount of sense. After all, the ideas of ghosts almost always find their roots in dark places. In the shadows of old creaky houses, in moonlit graveyards and abandoned buildings—places that lie in the deep, dark thrall of whatever heavy past hangs over them. Not that the famous Florida theater doesn't have a history.

Designed by renowned theater architect John Eberson, the theater opened its doors to the public on October 15, 1926, and was instantly received as a monument to Tampa Bay's cultural scene. It is easy to understand why, even today. Gargoyles and a terrazzo floor in the lobby, an interior embellished by statues, tapestries, banners, copper, brass and terra-cotta—it is hard not to be impressed by the exaggerated lavishness of the building. And yet, as impressive as the building is, there was a time when it was almost lost. The theater's decline began in the 1950s, a direct result of the massive exodus of urban populations into the suburbs. Just like so many other cities across the United States at the time, Tampa's city center suffered.

The streets were emptied at night, and the once-bustling theater was reduced to a darkened hulk in the heart of a decrepit municipality. The building seemed destined to be torn down for parking space, and it may well have been, if not for a major restoration effort that began in the late 1970s. Spearheaded by Arts Council members, city officials and volunteers, the building was reopened to the public in 1977, revamped and ready for a bright future.

Today, the theater's near-demise is less than a memory. Possibly busier than it has ever been, the playhouse has resumed its place as the city's cultural center, offering world-class musical performances and regular screenings of the best movies the film industry has to offer. Week after week, the theater buzzes with audiences who have come to take in these cultural events—audiences who aren't too mindful of the theater's past, and even less aware of its resident ghost: Foster Fink Finley.

It is impossible to say how Fink feels about this general lack of interest. While he was alive, there was nothing about the man that suggested he was an attention-seeker. On the contrary, Foster Finley was a quiet man. Working in the projectionist's booth from 1930 to 1965, he labored without fuss or bother, day in and day out, for 35 years. It was said that he had a wife and family, but no one had ever met them, and Fink never volunteered any information. The Great Depression, Second World War, Korean War and the assassination of John F. Kennedy came and went—and through it all, Fink clocked in five days a week, loading and unloading film reels with a decades-long silence, his ever-present cigarette jutting from the corner of his mouth.

Then, in 1965, he stopped. Seized by a sudden chest pain midway through a movie, Foster wasn't able to finish his shift; he was driven home by one of his coworkers, and never returned to run another movie. Fink had suffered a heart attack that day, and was dead two months later. It was the end of an era for the Tampa Bay Theatre. The man who had operated the projection camera almost the entire time it had been open was gone. Almost as soon as he died, the slow decline of business at the theater really began to bottom out.

The theater became a dark, empty place, as though it had followed Fink to the grave. But in 1977, when extensive renovations led to the rebirth of its popularity among Tampa Bay theater-goers, it wasn't the only thing reborn.

Soon after the renovations were complete, strange stories began to circulate about the old building. Among the first were those told by Fink's former assistant projectionist. Having taken over the booth soon after Fink had passed, this man worked for years without issue. But after the renovations in 1977, he talked of strange things occurring in his tiny workroom in the back of the theater.

First, there was the matter of the projection room door. The first time he felt the tugging on the other side of the door when he went to close it, he assumed it was his assistant, trying to get in at the moment he was swinging it shut. Fink's successor immediately let go of the handle and called his assistant in, only to find that there was no one there. This occurred more than once, always before he was about to screen a film, but only when he was in the room by himself. It was only one of many unsettling reminders that things weren't as they seemed in the projection booth.

There was also the matter of the generator door. It suddenly seemed to have acquired a life of its own, opening and closing mid-film, at precisely the moment when the projectionists were watching for the cue to switch reels. Because they were concentrating on the movie whenever this occurred, neither the projectionist nor his assistant had ever actually seen the door open and close. But they heard it: the door knob turning, the booth flooded by the sound of the humming generator, and the door swinging shut before either of them were able to turn around. Stories of these experiences quickly got out. When the power switches in the booth began to switch off on their own, people couldn't help but think of Fink Finley. It couldn't be denied that the weird goings-on seemed to be focused on the projection room. Had the renovations somehow woken Fink's spirit?

At first, the weird incidents seemed to be confined to the projection booth, but it wasn't long before things were being reported all over the theater. Belongings of theater employees would mysteriously vanish and turn up in the strangest places. It wasn't long before employees linked these cases of petty thievery to whatever was playing games with the doors and power switches in the projection room. Some of the workers began speaking directly to the mischievous spirit in the theater, and often, it would respond.

There was the case of the custodian whose knife had vanished while he was cleaning up one evening. After spending several days looking for it, the exasperated man stood at the balcony and called into the empty theater, asking for his knife back. Turning then, he saw it—his knife, on the floor, propped against the wall near the projection booth.

Along with the projectionist, this custodian was one of the early believers in the ghost of Fink Finley. According to him, all sorts of bizarre things went on when he was working in the theater by himself. While mopping the lobby, he was often interrupted by a tapping on his shoulder. But every time he spun around to look, there were only the gargoyles and an empty room behind him. As startling as the shoulder tapping was initially, the man eventually grew accustomed to it, and after a while, he stopped turning to look, only muttering irritated oaths under his breath.

When the ghost increased his activities at the theater, the only thing the custodian could do was laugh. He was locking up the theater on a Sunday afternoon the first time he heard the sound—chains being dragged across the lobby's terrazzo floor. He knew there was no one in the theater, but he was aware of the chains right in front of him even though there were no chains in sight. Despite it all, the man just couldn't work himself into a fright. Chains were just too theatrical, cliché. The idea struck the custodian that the spirit at the Tampa Bay Theatre was desperate to be acknowledged. "Have your fun, Fink," the man called into the lobby. "I've got to finish up my work and head home."

By this time, the custodian and the projectionist truly believed they were dealing with Fink Finley. They believed that he'd returned after the renovations, and for whatever reason, was seeking something that he never seemed to want while he was alive: attention. Did he want people to know he was displeased with the changes to the theater he'd helped run for so many years? Or maybe he was able to witness the theater's resurgence and wanted to be a part of its second golden age? It is impossible to say, but the custodian and the projectionists weren't the only ones to become aware of his presence.

Every now and then, accounts would come from others, theater-goers and employees alike. There were cold spots on the lobby staircase, accompanied by sudden inexplicable jolts of fear. Others spoke of a moving figure flashing in the mirrors of the front auditorium. And then there were the stories of people hearing the opening music of the Looney Tunes cartoon faintly playing in the lobby. Was Fink a Bugs Bunny fan?

The story of Fink Finley's ghost eventually got out among paranormal enthusiasts, and in 1984, one group endeavored to conduct a séance in the main auditorium. Though the channeling session offered no concrete proof of the former projectionist's presence, all in the circle later said that they definitely "felt" the presence of another being, that they were all seized by a feeling of being watched.

If Fink actually does haunt the Tampa Theatre—if this "someone" watching truly is the ghost of Fink Finley, then maybe the sad question that follows is: who is watching Fink? Certainly not the bulk of the theater's customers. To this day, the odd story emerges of someone being hit with an inexplicable blast of cold on the lobby stairs. Someone else might feel a tapping on his back in the middle of a movie and turn to find an empty seat behind them.

Occurring anywhere else, such accounts would definitely hitch a place with a haunted reputation, but all
things considered, Fink doesn't get much attention at the
Tampa Theatre. Fact is, these weird goings-on are overshadowed by the movies and live music that are featured
regularly. Fink doesn't really have a chance. Billing some
of the best live musicians in the business on its stage and
the most-talked about cinematic releases on its screen, the
old Florida theater manages to keep its audience's attention fixed on the show. The present simply overwhelms
the past at the Tampa Theatre. If Fink is hoping to get the
attention in the afterlife that he didn't get while he was
living, he definitely picked the wrong building to haunt.

5
Ghosts in Public Places

Cemeteries of St. Augustine

"One of the things I most like to do when I travel is check out the cemeteries," says Shelly Dingle of western Florida. "A lot of people say, 'Shelly, that's just so weird!' I've always liked to explore different places that way, though. A lot of history, and clues about the people that used to live there, can be found in a place's cemeteries. Every cemetery has so much to tell."

A number of these histories, Shelly admits, aren't the kind you read about in textbooks. "I guess it is obvious about graveyards and ghosts," she says. "A lot of graveyards, especially the old ones, are full of ghost stories. To be honest, that is what got me interested in the first place. It was fun when I was younger, visiting the local graveyard with friends at night, making noises and then saying, 'Did you hear that?!' Or pretending that we saw something. Every now and then, I'd convince myself that maybe I *had*. But looking back, it was always just hopeful thinking."

Hopeful thinking? What makes a ghost sighting something to hope for?

"I don't know, there has always been a part of me that hoped to see a ghost on one of those nights," Shelly continues. "Even now, whenever I get the chance to travel, see a new graveyard, I have this thought in the back of my head that maybe this time around, something will rise out of one of the tombstones. The way graveyards look, the way they feel—I walk through them sometimes and it just feels like there *should* be ghosts."

Shelly is definitely not alone in this assertion. Cemeteries suggest ghosts to people everywhere. Paranormal investigators across the country choose cemeteries as the sites for the bulk of their investigations. Practically every town and every city from Maine to California boasts at least one graveyard where the spirits of the dead are said to lurk. One of the most common settings for ghost stories and supernatural folktales, cemeteries are, and always have been, the cultural space where the land of the living meets the province of the dead. All across the country there are people like Shelly Dingle, who are fascinated with visiting American burial grounds in hopes that something wispy and spectral will rise from one of the gravestones. And, as with most everything of popular interest in the American marketplace, there is a service that caters to that demand— the ghost tour.

Shelly explains: "Usually in a ghost tour you are guided through an old area where the ghost may be living. The guides usually know a lot about the local history, and on the tour, of course, you learn the history of the haunted places. Most of the tours I've taken are at night, and pass through a cemetery."

Usually, whenever Shelly visits somewhere new, the local ghost tours are one of the first things she looks into. "Some places are more famous for their ghost tours than others," she says. "There are the obvious examples, like New Orleans, where there are cemeteries full of these beautiful mausoleums and a great story about each one. Ghosts are big in New Orleans, and there are a lot of people who go there just to soak it all in, firsthand. The ghost tours there, just like the cemeteries, are amazing."

Though Shelly herself has been to the Big Easy on more than one occasion, and taken every trip through every cemetery and purportedly haunted house open to the public, she has never seen a ghost. "Never once," she says. "Not just in New Orleans, but I've been to other graveyards, as well. I took a tour through Gettysburg, which everyone says is haunted. I've been to the Stull Cemetery in Kansas City. I even went up to the Resurrection Cemetery in Chicago once, where it seems like everyone and his dog talks about the ghost of Resurrection Mary. Didn't see a thing."

Shelly states that, though she never lost her fascination for cemeteries, after a while it started to become more of an academic interest rather than that visceral thrill that had initially pulled her in. "I started to examine the way cemetery architecture has changed over time, or the lay-out of graveyards, and the different ways people are buried according to their religious beliefs and their own personal ideas. For a while, cemeteries stopped being about ghosts."

That was until her trip to St. Augustine, the self-proclaimed oldest city in the United States. "St. Augustine is a city that is really proud of its history," Shelly says. "And it should be. It dates back very far, but I didn't really ever consider visiting for the longest time. Boy, was I ever glad I did when I finally got around to it."

On a summer trip, Shelly made arrangements to go on the town's ghost tour soon after she was settled. "I remember that night really clearly," she says. "The air was charged and everyone in the tour felt it. The city was old and beautiful and I was really looking forward to walking

St. Augustine Huguenot Cemetery

around." Shelly is quick to point out that she was only feeling her familiar old thrill of stomping through grave-yards at night; she'd felt it numerous times before. There was nothing that led her to believe that the night would bring her a ghostly run-in of her own. But that night, in St. Augustine's Huguenot Cemetery, Shelly's lifelong wish of coming face-to-face with a ghost was going to come true.

Established in 1821 to accommodate a yellow fever epidemic, the Huguenot Cemetery was distinct for being the only Protestant burial ground in all of St. Augustine at the time. Because the Catholic Church wouldn't hold funeral services for deceased Protestants, those who were buried in Huguenot during its early years were interred in humble plots. It became known as a cemetery for St. Augustine's rootless, those recent arrivals that were far from home, without church, friends or family.

Surely, those familiar with the stories surrounding the Huguenot might not be too surprised to hear that this is where Shelly finally had her long-awaited supernatural encounter. Given the sheer number of ghost sightings reported in the St. Augustine cemetery, some might say that if a person were to see a ghost anywhere, Huguenot would be the place.

Without a doubt, the honorable old Judge John Stickney is the cemetery's most famous spirit. Appointed County Judge of St. Johns, Stickney arrived in St. Augustine shortly after the Civil War, a widower with three children. He contracted typhoid during an 1882 business trip to Washington D.C. and died later that year in the nation's capital, but his children had his body shipped to St. Augustine, where he was laid to rest in the Huguenot Cemetery.

But that was not the end of his story; the former judge was destined to be one of those few unfortunate corpses subjected to a fair bit of posthumous travel. His body was called upon to make another trip to Washington D.C. over 20 years later, in 1903. The judge's children had relocated back to the capital and decided that they wanted their father's remains close by. Some believe that it was the humiliation which he endured then, while being dug up from the Florida earth, that brought his restless spirit back from the grave.

The undertakers had just pulled the judge's coffin from the ground when a gang of thieves descended upon the gravesite. Frightening the gravediggers away, the robbers tore off the lid of the coffin to see what valuables they could relieve John Stickney of. There, wedged into the judge's skull, was a spectacular row of gold teeth gleaming under the glow of the robbers' upraised lanterns. What need does a dead man have of teeth? It's doubtful that any of the grave robbers bothered asking themselves that question, though the answer would've certainly justified the haste in which they relieved the skeleton of its precious chompers. They disappeared into the night, leaving the rest of the body untouched.

Well, anybody who knows anything about such matters knows that disinterring a dead body is one surefire way of upsetting a spirit at rest. But stealing his teeth? Even in death, Judge Stickney wouldn't dream of bearing such an indignity without raising a fuss.

And so, ever since that fateful night, the ghost of the old St. Johns County Judge has acquired the habit of getting up and wandering around, searching the shadows of the Huguenot Cemetery at night for his golden teeth. Or so the locals say. It is as good an explanation as any for the dark figure that has been spotted there at night ever since. Appearing in a tall hat and long black cape, the figure is always seen walking around with a stoop, looking down at the ground as he goes, hoping to stumble upon, or so it is thought, a glimmer of gold in the grass.

There is reason to believe, however, that after nearly a century of searching, the judge has become a little discouraged by the seemingly endless hunt. Throughout the

1990s, people began spotting the man, wearing his top hat and cape, sitting in the cedar tree above his burial monument. Quietly looking around the cemetery with a morose, toothless expression, the judge usually appears for no more than a few minutes before vanishing from sight. His favorite perch in the tree, a stout cedar branch, once hung not too high from the ground. In 1999, when Hurricane Floyd swept through St. Augustine and tore Stickney's favorite branch off the tree, he simply relocated to another branch, higher up. Apparently, the former patriarch now has quite the elevated vantage point over his graveyard. Still no teeth though.

"I thought it was a charming little story," Shelly Dingle says of the ghostly legend that the tour guide recounted as they walked through the graveyard. "And so did everyone else in the group. A few people chuckled at the idea of this poor, toothless judge searching the graveyard for his teeth, and then retreating up his tree, maybe to sulk. It was kind of ridiculous, if you think about it." Shelly pauses before continuing. "Then again, I think a lot of us were chuckling just to hear our voices. It was actually kind of creepy in that cemetery. The story was one thing, but some people were whispering to each other. They were talking about sounds they thought they could hear. No doubt, a lot of us were jumpy. There was definitely something about that place that got to you." Shelly confesses the feeling was so real that some part of her expected the judge's ghost to appear in the cedar above his burial monument, staring down at their assembled party with a sad look.

But despite the weird feeling in the cemetery, despite the sense that something in the darkness was watching them, the boughs of the cedar tree were unoccupied. "I was disappointed and relieved about it at the same time," Shelly says. "I guess John Stickney must have felt fine being toothless that night."

Then the weird feeling Shelly spoke of got stronger. "We were in front of three tombstones that looked almost identical," Shelly explains, "and the tour guide was saying something about how these three guys, all of them young men, died at about the same time, all within the same month in the 1830s. Suddenly, I got this really cold, cold feeling up my back and down my arms."

Shelly, standing at the back of the group, suddenly found herself feeling vulnerable with her back to the graveyard. "The first time I looked over my shoulder, I thought for sure there had been someone standing there. I felt it in my gut." She shot another quick look over her shoulder. "Even though I couldn't see anything, I was convinced—no—let me correct that, I *knew* that there was something there."

Shelly turned back to the tour but wasn't able to concentrate. The cold crawling up her back was getting worse. She turned to look again. And there it was.

"That was when I saw her. She was standing so close I almost jumped out of my skin," Shelly says. "She was right beside me. This woman with black, black hair down her back, just standing, looking ahead at nothing, really, a totally blank expression on her face." Though the sight of the woman made her stomach churn, though she was hit by a sudden urge to turn and run, all she could do was stand and stare.

"I'm sure my mouth was hanging open. I was in total shock; I couldn't breathe or make a sound. She looked real enough for me to reach out and touch her, but I couldn't even get myself to blink." Shelly describes the woman as wearing an antiquated off-white dress. "It wasn't some big poofy number from 100 years ago or anything—just an old-fashioned dress like something my mother would have worn in the '50s. She looked like she could've been in her 40s or something, though I couldn't say for sure. She might have been a very pretty woman, but her skin was chalk-white and the look on her face was so lifeless it made my skin crawl."

Shelly isn't able to say for sure how long she stood there in mute shock next to the silent apparition. "It could have been a few seconds or a few minutes. It was just the two of us standing there. Everyone else was listening to the tour guide, and I was the only one who knew she was there." Snapped out of her trance by the end of the tour guide's story about the three identical gravestones, Shelly looked away for a second as the rest of the group began moving on. When she looked back, the woman was gone.

"When I think about it now," Shelly says, "I should have said something. But I was still in so much shock, I don't know if I could have put it into words. It's funny. It isn't like when you're a kid and goofing off about all the things you're pretending to see and hear. The second I was looking the real thing in the face, I just froze. I couldn't say a word. Looking back, it's too bad. I'm sure some of those people on that tour would like to have known how close they were to a real ghost."

That wasn't all there was to the tour. After that, the group made its way to the Tolomato Cemetery down the street. "I have to hand it to the guide," Shelly says. "She did a great job. She really knew her stuff, and was a great story-teller. She took us through the Tolomato, where she told us about the Bridal Ghost, an apparition of a lady dressed all in white. After what I'd seen in the Huguenot, you can imagine how jumpy I was. Every tombstone and tree branch was spooking me out. It was great. I felt like I was in high school again."

Shelly wasn't the only one. The group was obviously taken with the story of the Bridal Ghost. They jumped at shadows as they made their way through the Tolomato by the light of the guide's lantern. Something about the idea of a dead bride wandering through the graveyard sparked the group's imagination, and there were even a few star-tled exclamations.

All of these, however, turned out to be false alarms, inspired by the way a tree or burial monument appeared from a certain angle. At one point, one of the group mem-bers mistook another for the storied apparition. No one saw the Bridal Ghost that night. Neither did they see the mysterious light that is said to occasionally shine from the chapel mortuary. The guide told them the story of the long-deceased Franciscan missionary named Father Corpa who had been murdered on the cemetery grounds after insulting an Indian who he had recently converted. One of the regular apparitions said to appear in the ceme-tery, a male figure in a black robe, is believed to be the spirit of this dead monk. Though the guide's story caused more than one group member to start at a shape that could have been an imagined black clad figure in the distance, no one that night could say they had a definitive sighting.

In fact, unless there were others in the group who had seen an apparition and kept quiet about it, the only person who was sure she saw a ghost that night was Shelly Dingle. "A lot has changed for me since that night," Shelly says. "All it takes is one experience like that. I'm a believer now, there's no doubt about that. I think about it a lot of the time. You know, if there are ghosts in Huguenot Cemetery, who is to say there aren't ghosts in other graveyards? Who is to say there are not spirits all over the place? Anything seems possible now." Needless to say, Shelly's fascination with the graveyards of America has increased considerably since her experience in St. Augustine. "I try not to talk about it too much. Let's face it, that sort of hobby makes people think twice about you. But yeah, you can call me a ghost-nut now. And next time I see one standing right beside me, you can bet I'm not going to just stand there and stare. I've got a few questions to ask."

The Walls of the Castillo de San Marcos

Dolores Marti would have done better not to wear such a distinctive perfume or, for that matter, so much of it. Everything clicked for Colonel Garcia Marti the moment the smell of his wife's perfume assaulted his senses as he sat at his desk one fateful afternoon in St. Augustine's stone fortress, over 200 years ago. It hit the colonel like a slap in the face when his subordinate, Captain Manuel Abela, leaned over his shoulder to clarify something in a report he had just submitted. The smell of his wife's perfume was all over Abela's uniform.

In an instant, everything was clear to him—how different his wife had become since he'd been stationed at the Castillo de San Marcos, her long absences, her near-constant preoccupation, her bright disposition. She was seeing this man, this Captain Abela, behind his back. He knew it beyond any doubt. With the flood of realization came a torrent of rage, and for a moment, it threatened to overwhelm him.

Then his instincts took over, and cold, hard reason put out the blaze. Colonel Marti forced himself to be calm. He was a senior officer of the Spanish Crown, after all. He hadn't risen to his rank by acting on impulse, without deliberation. Marti swallowed hard, the dangerous light in his eyes the only evidence of the fire inside. After Captain Abela was done clarifying his report, Marti nodded curtly, thanked him and then dismissed the man.

Castillo de San Marcos

Captain Abela saluted and strode out of the colonel's office, completely unaware of the terrible chain of thoughts that were forming in the colonel's mind.

Soldiers at the fort began to ask questions fairly quickly. The captain hadn't answered muster for several days, and he was nowhere to be found. Abela, with his quick and easy laugh, had always been one of the more popular officers among the men. After several days, the fort was buzzing with whispers about his absence. When Colonel Marti finally addressed his men about the captain, it was with an air of slight surprise and mild rebuke. After reminding them that it was not becoming for soldiers of the Crown to question the strategies of their superiors, the colonel agreed to tell his men about the captain to put their skittish minds at ease. He announced that captain Abela had been assigned to an urgent mission in Cuba, and that he had left without a word because the success of his assignment depended upon secrecy. Thus ended all questions regarding the whereabouts of Captain Manuela Abela.

It took a little bit longer for the same curiosity about Dolores Marti to seize the fort. Among the soldiers, it would have been considered improper, to say the least, to confront the colonel with questions about his wife. Even when they spoke about her amongst themselves, they did so with lowered voices lest anyone of any rank or inflated sense of propriety overhear. For the families in St. Augustine who considered themselves friends of the colonel and his wife, it was a different matter. Though they too wondered at the sudden absence of the young woman, they found that Colonel Marti had become most difficult to communicate with. He'd taken to wearing a dark, glowering expression wherever he went, and met every casual greeting with a withering glare. In town, people grew concerned about the situation. Why didn't Dolores leave the house anymore? And why did the colonel look like he was always one breath away from challenging every greeting with a duel?

Colonel Marti was hardly oblivious to these whisperings, and everyone was shocked the day he invited all his friends to a dinner at his house. Overflowing with curiosity, everyone who received an invitation showed up, but if they were expecting to have husband and wife greet them at they door, they were disappointed. Colonel Marti received them without Dolores, sitting alone at the head of the table. Knowing full well that the question of his wife's whereabouts was the reason everyone had come; he addressed the issue as soon as all of his guests were present.

He stood up before dinner was served and, with that same somber expression that everyone had come to know over the past weeks, informed the dinner party that Dolores was in need of their prayers. The heat and humidity of St. Augustine had not agreed with her. She'd fallen ill, he said, and after much deliberation, he had decided to send her to Mexico where her aunt would nurse her back to health. After she recovered, god willing, she would return home to Spain, where the climate was much more suited to her gentle constitution.

Right after Marti had finished telling his story, the room was full of concern and sympathy. The guests assured the colonel that they would pray for Dolores' recovery every day. Some cursed St. Augustine for its climate, insisting that no civilization could ever be expected to flourish in such a place. They gave him their condolences and their best wishes. The colonel took it all with gracious silence, his somber look now tinged with modest gratitude.

But in the following days, it became obvious that no one had really believed a lot of what the colonel had said. The last time any of them had seen her, Dolores had seemed to be in perfect health. If she actually were ill, had her illness been so bad that she couldn't manage a simple good-bye to anyone she'd known in St. Augustine? Not even her closest friends were given the benefit of a farewell before she'd vanished.

Numerous theories began to circulate. Some surmised that there was no sickness, but that the colonel's lively young wife couldn't bear the quiet life in the colony and had run off back to Spain without telling anyone. Others suggested it wasn't the quiet life in the colony that had driven her away, but the colonel and his ice-cold temperament. As witty and charming as a woman could be, Dolores had always been quite the opposite of her dour and humorless husband. No one would have been overly surprised if they learned that she had run off to get away from the oppressive Colonel Marti. Of course, there were those who brought up the missing captain, Manuel Abela, whose disappearance coincided uncannily with Dolores'. There had always been talk about how well the pair had gotten along; some enjoyed speculating at the possibility of an affair. Could the colonel's announcements about Captain Abela's urgent mission to Cuba and his wife's illness have been an attempt to cover up his shame about the affair?

No one was ever able to provide the definitive answer to the question of what happened to Dolores, but few would dare to consider the explanation that would emerge nearly 50 years later.

A lot had changed by 1833. The Castillo de San Marcos and the Florida Territory on which it stood was now part of the United States. The mystery surrounding Dolores, Colonel Marti and Captain Abela had long been relegated from local gossip to historical curiosity. All those who had spent time guessing what had truly happened between Colonol Marti, Dolores and Captain Abela had passed away. Surely each and every one of them would have been

Dungeons below Castillo de San Marcos

shocked at the discovery made by a United States engineer, Lieutenant Stephen Tuttle.

On July 21, 1833, Lieutenant Tuttle was taking a look around the dungeons beneath the old stone fort. While studying the structural layout of the place, he stumbled on one section of wall that made him hesitate. He tapped it and found that it sounded hollow. Perhaps he had visions of hidden Spanish gold dancing in his head when he took a hammer to the mortar and began chipping away. But it wasn't gold that he found sealed away in the dungeon wall.

A flowery smell filled the hall when he removed the first stone block. It was strong, nearly overpowering, and Tuttle actually looked over his shoulder at one point, thinking that maybe a woman with a fondness for perfume might have approached. But the hall was empty, lit only by the dim glow of his lantern. He went back to work on the wall—chipping mortar, removing stone blocks—until the hidden treasure he imagined revealed itself to be something else all together. There, entombed within the wall, were two skeletons propped up side by side.

Word of the Lieutenant's find got out quickly, and it wasn't long before those with a tendency for storytelling began to talk about Dolores, Captain Abela and the jealous husband who had them killed and sealed them inside the walls of his dungeon. Were they sealed up into the wall alive, or had they already been dead? Did he do the deed himself, or were there others in on the plot? It seemed there were as many answers to these questions as there were storytellers. And the stories didn't stop there.

Bizarre reports began to emerge from the depths of the Castillo de San Marcos. People spoke of a strange light they saw shining against the wall where the two skeletons had been dug up. Others who walked down that hall told of an overpowering perfume that would suddenly fill the dank confines of the passageway—sometimes barely noticeable, other times so strong it teetered on oppressive.

According to current accounts, this smell hasn't dissipated much with the years. Tour guides taking people through the dungeons of the Castillo de San Marcos make a point to stop at the spot where the bones were found. Sometimes, as a group approaches, a dim glow can be seen emanating from the wall. Often, tour guides will stop there and tell the story of the two dead lovers. To this day, it isn't uncommon to have the tale punctuated by a strong flowery smell that fills the hall.

Could this mean that Delores Marti remains in the dungeon, her spirit forever bound inside the rock where she was sealed? Or is this smell some sort of psychic residue, an impression of the last thing Captain Abela sensed as he was being entombed with the colonel's wife? And what, exactly, is the dim light that some claim to have seen? We can only guess, and perhaps ponder the issue of crime and according punishment. For if the couple is indeed still tied to the stone and the darkness of the ancient fort, maybe someone ought to tell them that they have done more than their fair share of time, and maybe it's time to go.

The Dormitory Ghosts of Ringling

The banging on the wall woke Kathy with a start. At first, she just lay there, hoping that she'd imagined it. A moment passed, and she stared into the darkness. The silence was tense, heavy, and she tried to convince herself that there had been no banging. *I imagined it,* she told herself. *No thanks to Anna and all her weird talk. Now she's got me jumping awake in the middle of the night. Honestly!*

Letting out an indignant huff, Kathy was about to roll over onto her side when another bang sounded against the wall. Her blood ran cold. "Anna?" she whispered to no one in the darkness, knowing there was no way her friend could hear her. Anna was sleeping in the next room— Room 210. Kathy shuddered at the sound of another bang. *Poor Anna. Room 210. What terrible luck.*

Though her heart was pounding in fear, she rolled out of bed, and as quietly as she could, made her way out of her room, careful not to wake her roommate. Anna had told Kathy about her fears in confidence. She didn't want it to get around that she suspected something wasn't quite right in her room. Kathy understood. People wouldn't react well if Anna started to talk about weird feelings in her room, especially after what had happened there. "What terrible luck," Kathy whispered to herself as she quietly closed the door behind her and approached the door of Room 210.

Another bang, this one faint, like something inside the room had fallen to the floor. Kathy felt a chill move up her back as she slid the key Anna had given her into the door and turned the knob. She did her best to ignore the goose bumps on her neck and arms, opened the door and took a step inside.

For a second, all she could do was stare, her reasoning unable to match what her eyes were seeing. There, in the darkness of the room, Anna and her roommate hovered in the air, about two feet above their beds. The young women were still asleep under their blankets, which hung over them. Kathy caught the gasp in her throat. Her feet were frozen in place; all she could do was stand and stare, one word repeating itself over and over in her mind: *Impossible.*

And then it got cold. It got very cold, and the darkness of the room became darker. Kathy grew conscious of the footsteps in the room. There was someone else there. Someone? No. Some*thing.* She saw it then, a black shadow, even blacker than the rest of the room. It moved toward her, a vague human shape coming closer, reaching out. Kathy let out a terrified shriek and turned and ran, tearing past her room and down the hall, waking up everyone as she ran, including Anna and her roommate. They had no recollection of their little levitating act.

So went another ghostly sighting in the first dormitory of the Ringling School of Art and Design—one ghostly sighting among many in the troubled history of the old Sarasota building. Kathy and Anna could be representative of any of the girls that stayed at the dormitory in the school years that followed 1977. Before the dorm was converted to the Keating Center, the administrative building it is today, several girls encountered with the spirit—and none of them were pleasant encounters.

Originally the Bay Haven Hotel, the dormitory was renovated in 1931 when Sarasota patriarch John Ringling opened up the city's now-celebrated school. The dormitory's macabre backstory finds its roots in 1929, when the building was still a hotel, with an unhappy young woman whose name has faded with time.

No one can say what her last name was, but her first name was either Mary or Belle, depending on who is telling the story. We can only guess what was troubling this young woman, but staying at the Bay Haven Hotel could have hardly helped. In the four years that it was open, the hotel garnered a sleazy reputation, and whatever dodgy activities occurred there took their toll on the young woman. In 1929, she hanged herself in the stairway, between the second and third floor. Fearful that word of the woman's suicide would be bad for business, the Bay Haven's owner kept it quiet, boarding up the staircase where she'd killed herself.

It wasn't until two years later, when Ringling's renovators were transforming the hotel into a dorm, that they discovered the skeleton in the boarded-up staircase. Soon after her discovery, all sorts of bizarre occurrences were reported by the first students to attend Ringling. There were accounts of personal possessions being picked up by invisible hands and moved across rooms, floating through the air right in front of bewildered students. Aspiring artists alone in their studios claimed to see paintbrushes stirring themselves in containers of water. Others spoke of an eerie-looking woman with pale skin and a jerky gait walking the halls by herself. This woman was only said to appear in students' peripheral vision, existing only in the corner of the eye. Whenever anyone tried to look directly at her, she vanished.

From the very beginning, Mary's (or Belle's) manifestations were a fairly regular occurrence at the Ringling dormitory, and for the most part, those students who she appeared before learned how to deal with her. She wasn't a malicious spirit, after all. Unsettling as it was to spy her moving through the halls, lifting random items or playing with paintbrushes, she never really harmed anyone. She seemed only to be visible to a small number of students, and a number of women who stayed in the dormitory would complete their schooling at Ringling swearing that she didn't exist.

Thus Mary (or Belle) became one of the unofficial students staying in the dorm, appearing often enough over the years to remain a hushed topic of conversation, yet not so often that she was considered a problem. The spirit in Room 210, however, was another matter altogether. According to Kim Cool, author of *Ghost Stories of Sarasota* (2003), more than one student sleeping there experienced things that they would do their best to forget.

It happened in 1977—the second suicide in the Ringling dormitory, a student found dead in her room, Room 210. If the spirit of Mary (or Belle) had made life at the dorm a bit spooky for some, it became a nightmare for the girl living in the haunted room.

A far more active spirit than the woman who took her own life in 1929, the ghost of Room 210 could be guaranteed to make life downright scary for those who were lodged in her room. Apparently, some students sensed it the moment they walked into the room for the first time—the still, cold air, the muffled way the light fell across the walls. Room 210 just felt wrong, and for those unfortunate enough to be staying there, more often than not, the feeling worsened.

It always came out at night. That was when the temperature in the room would drop, the shadows would deepen, and something in the room would come to life—something dark and spiteful and not at all happy about having to share its room. Some students picked up on the presence better than others, complaining of the chill in the room, harboring secret fears about turning out the light—and with good reason.

It wasn't uncommon for these students to wake up and find themselves staring at a dark figure standing at the edge of their beds. Others were plagued by banging noises on their walls when they were alone, and some had their possessions picked up and tossed across the room. A few awoke to find that they themselves were being picked up, hovering one or two feet over their beds only to be dropped down the moment they were able to register what was going on. Well, none of the students who had the misfortune of staying in Room 210 came to Ringling with the intention of including paranormal encounters as part of their education, and all who experienced these things wasted no time finding another room.

The increased incidence of paranormal phenomena wasn't limited to Room 210. Kim Cool spoke to a former Ringling student named Tim Jaeger, who relates a personal experience in the dormitory: "I was a teaching assistant at Ringling at the time," he says. "One day I heard a scream. It was very early in the morning. A lady cleaning in the bathroom had seen a reflection in the mirror, but there was no one there."

According to Jaeger, the vision in the mirror sent the woman into hysterics, and she quit her job on the spot. While this woman wasn't the only custodian to spot an apparition while cleaning, it seems as though there may have been more than one spirit that frequented the washroom. For every sighting terrible enough to send witnesses into a panic, there was another encounter that suggested nothing more than benign mischief. The unfortunates who ran into the former described a bone-white woman with long black hair and a look of utter loathing stretched across her dead face. All who laid eyes on this woman had one thing in common: a fierce and sudden terror. The first instinct was to cut and run, and there were few who ignored it.

Yet, is seems there was a gentler spirit present as well. This ghost seemed to enjoy tormenting the building's custodians, tapping their shoulders as they mopped, or blowing icy cold breath over their ears and down their backs. Irritating to some, certainly, eerie to others, yes—but no one who encountered this spirit ever experienced anything resembling the terror the lady with the black hair elicited.

So it wasn't all suicides and bad-tempered spirits at the Ringling dormitory. In fact, there was one account that suggests a bit of spectral generosity. The story goes that there was one female student from up north who was leaving Sarasota to go home for Christmas holidays. Apparently, this girl was careful with her belongings and made sure that all her things were locked in her closet and locked behind her dorm room door before she left.

When she returned in January, the door to her room was still locked, but once inside, she instantly noticed that things were not how she had left them. Her closet door was ajar; someone had unlocked it while she was gone. Automatically assuming she'd been robbed, the girl crossed her room and flung the closet open. Much to her surprise, all her things were still inside, but out of place.

Her clothes and shoes had been slid to either sides of the closet, leaving a space in the middle where someone had left her an astonishing gift. Hanging there from the clothes rack was a perfectly preserved lace dress, dating back to the late 1920s. On the closet floor right underneath the garment was a pair of heeled silk shoes that matched the dress perfectly.

The dormitory's long record of strange stories came to an end when it was shut down and reestablished as the Keating Center, an administrative center for the school. Since the dorm rooms have been replaced by office space, there has been no word of the ghosts that were believed to haunt the building. Why is this? Maybe the latest round of renovations changed the building so much that the spirits felt they didn't belong there anymore. Perhaps the ghosts found that office workers are less fun to haunt than arts students, and left out of boredom.

Or maybe, just maybe, the ghostly girls are still there, but they shy away from all the bright light and pencil pushing that goes on in the daytime. It could be that they actually come out at night—the angry spirit from what used to be Room 210 and the friendlier ghost that killed herself on the staircase. Given that ghosts are often known to stick to the places they haunt for very long periods of time, we can only hope that, for their sake, the two spirits have a lot in common.

Ghost Stalker

"Don't call me an expert or anything, but I always thought ghosts were supposed to haunt places, not people," says "Joni Hoight," an anonymous resident of southeast Miami, who requests to go by a pseudonym. "Ghosts that haunt houses aren't really supposed to leave those houses, right? Usually something happened to them while they lived there a long time ago, and that is where they stay, scaring anyone who lives there. You move out of the house, and there should be no problems, right?"

This is the common theory, anyway. Haunted houses remain haunted regardless of who's living in them. People may come and go, but the ghosts remain. Anyone unlucky enough to be moving into a haunted house need only move, and the ghosts will be left behind. This is what the bulk of supernatural literature would have us believe, but it wouldn't be so simple for Ms. Hoight.

"Just over four years ago, I moved into this cool little apartment in South Miami," Joni begins. "It was as a character suite, a bit old, a bit of a fixer-upper, but I didn't mind. It was the first place I'd moved into on my own, and I was really excited about it. There was a lot of work to do, but I was happy about it, actually. I thought it was great that I'd be able to put together a place that was mine. My own."

But Joni hadn't been in her new apartment long when she started to get the impression that, although she was the only one paying the rent, she wasn't the sole occupant. "It started as soon as I started renovating," she says. "I got this feeling that there was someone or something else there, something that was working against me in all of its little ways."

Those familiar with paranormal phenomena will recognize some of the early happenings in Joni Hoight's apartment. "At first, I thought I was going crazy," she says. "Nails that I had just put down a second before would be gone when I reached for them. Tools and paintbrushes vanished by themselves off my kitchen counter. Twice, paint cans I placed on the floor were tipped over when I wasn't looking. There were a few times when I left to get some lunch, and when I got back, the radio was tuned in to a station I never listen to, and on full blast."

Things got so bad that by the time Joni was finished renovations, she was already thinking about moving. "What really sucked was that the place looked great, and I should have been so happy with the end result, but sitting back and enjoying it was the last thing on my mind. The more time went by, the more certain I became that there really was something else living there."

Something else?

"Okay, a ghost," Joni says. "I suppose it's funny that I still have problems saying that. I never really believed in that sort of thing, and truthfully, I still have days when I've got problems accepting what I went through. There are days when it all feels like a bad dream. A bad dream that went on for a long, long time."

As it turned out, Joni would never feel comfortable in her new apartment. "Weird things continued to happen after I was finished my renovations. Sometimes the lights would be switched on while I was asleep, and I'd notice when I got up the next morning. But there were other times when it was worse. I would be woken by the lights in the kitchen and the living room switching on and off really fast. From my bedroom, it looked like someone had set up a strobe light in my living room. I have to say, the flashing lights never stopped scaring the [expletive] out of me."

It didn't stop there. "There were footsteps in the hall all the time, night and day," Joni says. "Sometimes they kept me up all night. It got so bad that there were times when I'd yell at whatever it was to stop. A few times, it did, but most of the time, once it started, there was no stopping it until the sun came up." There are those who find ways to cope with spirits in their homes, but not Joni. Joni was an extremely unhappy tenant who never got used to the happenings in her apartment,. "I was having trouble sleeping at night, and I was too embarrassed to have people over. Friends were always asking to see the place— wondering when I was going to have my housewarming, but I couldn't get myself to talk about what was going on. I don't know why."

After three months in her new place, Joni decided that she'd had enough. "I ended up breaking my lease," she says, "but I didn't care. My thinking was, *get me out of this place, as quickly as possible.*" So it was that her landlord kept her lease payment and Joni moved out into the first affordable place she could find.

"The second place was nothing like the first," she says. "It was a really new apartment—small—one of those cookie cutter concrete places, linoleum floor and carpet. I wasn't crazy about it, that's for sure, but I looked at it as a place in between places, until I found something nicer." Much to her dismay, Joni soon found out that ghosts are just as likely to haunt drab concrete apartments as they are quaint character suites.

Even now, four years later, there is still a twinge of wonder in her voice when she recalls her experiences in her new place: "I couldn't believe it. I still can't believe it. All the same stuff that happened in my other place was happening in the new apartment, and more!" As well as the flickering lights and footsteps, her belongings started to vanish. "It was like it was in the beginning, when I was renovating the first place," she recalls, "but worse."

More than once, she was about to step out the door to go to work, only to discover that her purse was nowhere to be found. "It was crazy, because I'm not the kind of person to misplace things," she says. "My purse is always on the table by the door. That's where I have always put it—it was a habit." So, imagine her surprise when her missing purse appeared in kitchen cupboards, under chairs and even once in the fridge. "And it wasn't just my purse," she continues. "Keys, cutlery, clothes—all my stuff was being rearranged daily. There was always something missing. I could never settle down there. I could never get comfortable because I was always spending my time looking for something that I'd lost."

"There were a few days when I thought I was going crazy, and I thought about going to see someone," she says. "I'd ask myself, 'Two apartments in a row? What are the chances? Could I be imagining this? Could I be doing it myself?'"

Who knows? She may have convinced herself that this was the case, if the phenomenon had been a bit less extreme. But she killed all such thoughts the day she came home from work to find all of her kitchenware in the center of the floor in her living room. She'd watched television late the night before, and nothing had been on her living room floor when she'd gone to bed. That morning, she'd been far too rushed to empty out her kitchen cupboards. As crazy as she had suspected herself of being, Joni knew there was no way she was responsible for the mess.

Although convinced of her own sanity, Joni is quick to point out that after she announced she was moving out of her second apartment in less than a year, her friends began to think she was nuts. "I still hadn't told anyone what I was going through," she says.

Thinking that maybe distance would do the trick, Joni decided to get as far away from the previous two places as possible. "The third place I moved into was just south of Fort Lauderdale," she says. "Quite a little jaunt from where I'd been, but I guess I was hoping that whatever had followed me to my second place would lose interest in following me such a distance." She was wrong.

"I think I almost had a nervous breakdown on the first night, when I heard the footsteps in the hall," she remembers. "I yelled and shouted at it to stop, and it did that first night, but then it was back again the next." Along with moving her things around, playing with her light switches and leaving footsteps in the hallway, the spirit haunting her had also acquired a disturbing new habit: appearing in her bedroom as a big black shadow standing at her doorway. It would remain there for several seconds before taking three bold steps in and then vanishing before it reached her bed.

"It only happened twice," she says, "and then I got help. I wasn't going to face this on my own anymore, and I wasn't going to move again. Something had been following me around since I moved into that South Miami apartment, and it was time to talk to someone who could help."

Who did Joni call? "I'd never been a religious person," she says. "But then I'd never believed in ghosts, either. "I actually ended up going to a nearby church and talking to a priest. I knew right away that he was a good man, and I told him everything that I'd been through. When I think about it, I'm still amazed at his reaction. He didn't judge me, or laugh, or even doubt me in any way. He told me he would come over to my house the next day with incense and holy water, and would bless me and my home."

That night, Joni dealt with the ghost that had followed her across the city for the last time. "His shadow didn't appear to me like it had the previous two nights," she says, "but he kept busy walking up and down the hall for most of the night. He also switched the lights in the kitchen on and off four times." Joni didn't call out to the spirit that night, but instead grit her teeth and bore it, telling herself that this would be the last night she'd have to endure her tormenter. She was right.

"The priest came over the next day and said prayers in every room," she says. "He lit incense and sprayed holy water. Also, he said extra prayers in the hallway, the kitchen, the living room and in my bedroom. Then he blessed me, personally." Joni claims that she knew something had changed the moment the priest was done. "I just felt different," she says, "everything felt different. I'm not sure if I can explain it, but it was like this weight I'd been carrying was lifted. I'd been carrying it around for so long that I didn't even know it was there, but when it was gone, I felt ecstatic, cured."

Ever since that day, Joni has had no more run-ins with her ghostly stalker. Life for her has returned to the way it was, except for one notable difference. "I go to church on Sundays now," she says.

Cruz' Return

"I'm from a small town, the kind of place where people like talking about their neighbors. Once a guy is known for something around here, that's it, you're stuck with it. Your reputation is your name. If word got out about the kind of things that have been happening in my backyard, I hate to think what they'd start calling me. Rather no one heard about it at all." And yet, given the sort of phenomena this small-town Floridian claims to be experiencing, it comes as something of a surprise that his neighbors don't yet know about it. Nevertheless, concern for his reputation keeps the man from revealing his name and the town where he is from.

"It all started about five months ago," he begins, "right after my dog died. I had two of them, but Cruz was the older fella. Can't say for sure how many years old he was, but for sure he had been around longer than some of the kids around here." The man had just buried Cruz two days previous, and was still trying to get used to his house, minus a companion. "I've always had dogs," he says, "but losing one never gets easier. It had been two days, and I was still moping around the house. Anyone who has ever lost a dog would know what I'm talking about. The place felt empty—whenever my other dog, Matt, came around, he just reminded me of Cruz. Didn't help at all that Matt looked about as depressed as I was."

But the sullen dejection in the house would be broken by a weird and wild hope that night. "I woke up in front of the TV; it was really late. There was some guy yelling about an exercise machine on the TV, but I wasn't paying any attention. Something else had woken me—a dog barking." His first thought was that it had been Matt, until he looked over and saw his Labrador-Shepherd-cross standing next to him, staring toward the kitchen.

"Matt wasn't really the yapping type, and I knew by the way he was looking at the kitchen and whimpering that something had gotten his attention." He thought of Cruz, feeling an irrational surge of optimism. For just a moment, his sleep-muddled thoughts turned to his late companion, and he was convinced that Cruz was still alive. "I knew it didn't make any sense, but I jumped up off the couch all the same. Matt started whining, his tail wagging." His dog's excitement buoyed his own, and the man called out, "Cruz?"

"I felt dumb as soon as I did it," the man says, and poor Matt looked at me and then back at the kitchen and started barking like mad. It was my fault, I thought, and I just couldn't tell him to stop. He heard Cruz's name and thought that he was back."

He knelt down and calmed Matt. "I was just petting him, telling him it was okay. I figured I was hearing things or something, maybe dreaming, but it took some time to calm the boy down. He was growling and barking, it was a good two or three minutes until he stopped."

In the silence that followed, the man largely disregarded the barking he thought he'd heard earlier. "I was wide awake by then, and I just accepted that, sure, I dreamed it. Cruz was gone, it was crazy thinking that Cruz might be in the backyard, barking away. Not likely, right?"

Certainly not, but a moment later, another sharp bark sounded from the backyard, causing the man's blood to freeze. "I'd heard that bark for the last 10 years of my life," the man says. "I knew exactly who it was, even though I knew that there was no way it could be." Matt was wrestling with the same contradiction, barking and whimpering at the same time, scuttling behind his master's legs.

But the man was so startled and confused that he barely noticed how frightened his normally protective pet was. "I don't know if I was saying it out loud or just saying it in my head over and over: 'You're dead Cruz. You're dead. You're dead. I buried you. You're dead.'"

The dead dog in the backyard barked continually for about one minute before the man finally decided to act. "After I had pulled myself together and started for the back door, Matt turned and ran the other way. That wasn't like him at all. Between Matt and Cruz, Matt was always the feisty one. Never backed down from anything. Seeing him run like that spooked me even more."

Nevertheless, he marched resolutely through his kitchen and threw open the back door. "I almost shouted for Cruz, but thought better of it. The neighbors knew that he'd passed, and I didn't want anyone to think I'd lost my head, calling out at night for a dead dog."

Instead, he just called a tentative "Hello?" into the night. As soon as he did, the barking stopped. "There was nothing back there. I switched on the patio light and saw that the backyard was completely empty. I grabbed a flashlight and checked under the cars and behind the shed, but didn't see a thing."

Far from being relieved that there was no spectral version of his late pet lingering in his backyard, the sudden silence only exacerbated his unease. "Just because it was quiet didn't mean that everything was fine. It made things worse. The more time I spent in that backyard, the heavier the silence became. I don't know how to explain it, exactly, but I knew he was in the backyard. I couldn't see him, but Cruz was still there."

Then he heard it—panting coming from the darkness. "By the time ol' Cruz started panting, I can't say that I was even surprised. Was it weird? Sure. But with the feeling in my gut right then and there, I think it would've been weirder if *nothing* happened. Now, I was sure. Something weird—something really weird was going on in my backyard. My dog had come back from the dead."

At first, the man stood completely still at the sound of the panting. "I knew that he was dead. I'd buried him myself. But if what I was hearing was his ghost, I thought maybe I'd be able to see Cruz again. The idea of it got me excited. I wasn't frightened by it at all—I guess you could say I liked the idea. Cruz was back, it made me smile."

He called out to his dog, and then, just like he'd done countless times over the years, he got down on one knee and called his name, hoping to catch a glimpse of the animal he missed so much. "Well, he didn't come," the man says. "The second I called his name, the panting stopped; I knew he was gone." Things went back to normal. The dead quiet in his backyard suddenly lost its weight, and Matt came loping out to where the man was kneeling, panting and whimpering. That concluded Cruz's first visit. But it wasn't long before there was another. "That first time, he stayed outside, but after that, he managed to sneak in. The next time me and Matt had a run in with ol' Cruz, it was inside the house."

It was two days later, and the man was on his couch, dozing in front of the television. "After that night in the backyard, I had some time to think about what had happened, and I guess I figured that this was Cruz's way of saying 'bye' to me and Matt. Thanks for the good times, or something like that. I didn't think we'd ever hear from him again." When the man felt movement on the couch near his feet, he assumed it was Matt. "Both my dogs have a bad habit of jumping up on the couch when I fall asleep there. I am always yelling at them about it."

Without bothering to open his eyes, the man hollered at Matt, calling his dog by name, ordering him to get off the couch. "Well, imagine my surprise when the critter on the couch started barking back at me! What surprised me even more was that it wasn't Matt barking. I'd know that bark anywhere. It was Cruz again."

Jolted from his slumber, the man sprung from the couch to stare wide-eyed at the spot on the couch where he'd felt the dog stir. It appeared that his ghostly pet was quicker than he—there was nothing there. "He wasn't on the couch anymore, but I could hear paws running across the kitchen floor. Matt started yelping like crazy at the backdoor, and I ran out back as fast as I could."

He made it into the kitchen just in time to see the screen door slam shut and Matt come running past him and into the living room, where he lay cowering in a corner. "I went running out to the backyard again. This time I called out loud. Nothing happened. I grabbed my flashlight and searched every corner. He didn't want to answer, though. He was there. I could feel it, but he wasn't answering."

The man said he stayed out there, wandering back and forth with his flashlight, whispering his dog's name, for over a quarter of an hour. Only when Matt appeared, whimpering anxiously on the back porch, did he give up his search. "When I went back inside that night, I had the feeling that Cruz was back to stay. I don't know how or why, but he didn't want to leave us. I guess he was having as much trouble letting go as we were."

The visits only increased over the next few weeks. "Cruz got so regular at our place that even Matt started getting used to it. He stopped getting spooked when Cruz would start yapping in the backyard. There were times when I was on the couch and I could feel that Cruz was there, too. Sometimes I could feel his weight on my legs, other times I could hear him panting away on the floor beside me."

Matt went from running out of the room whenever this would happen to gradually accepting the ghostly presence of his former playmate. "It wasn't too long before I noticed Matt playing around in a room all by himself," the man says. "He was never the kind of dog to chase his own tail, and I got to thinking that he was actually playing around with ol' Cruz. That, or old age was starting to get to his head."

The man claims that the spirit of Cruz has moved right in with himself and Matt, and it shows no signs of moving on. "Let me put it this way," the man says. "I haven't gone so far as to start filling his food and water bowls, but," he's quick to add, "I haven't gotten rid of them either, and I don't intend to, as long as his ghost is kicking around."

GHOST HOUSE BOOKS

Collect the Entire Series of Ghost House Books!

Canada
- ❑ 1. Ghost Stories and Mysterious Creatures of British Columbia
- ❑ 3. More Ghost Stories of Alberta
- ❑ 4. Ghost Stories of Manitoba
- ❑ 5. More Ghost Stories of Saskatchewan
- ❑ 6. Ontario Ghost Stories
- ❑ 8. Ghost Stories of the Maritimes
- ❑ 9. Even More Ghost Stories of Alberta
- ❑ 10. Canadian Ghost Stories

United States
- ❑ 1. Ghost Stories of Washington
- ❑ 3. Ghost Stories of California
- ❑ 4. Ghost Stories of Hollywood
- ❑ 5. Ghost Stories of Illinois
- ❑ 6. Ghost Stories of Texas
- ❑ 7. Ghost Stories of Michigan
- ❑ 8. Ghost Stories of Indiana
- ❑ 9. Ghost Stories of Minnesota
- ❑ 10. Ghost Stories of Ohio

General
- ❑ 2. Ghost Stories of the Rocky Mountains
- ❑ 11. Ghost Stories of Christmas
- ❑ 12. Haunted Christmas
- ❑ 13. Haunted Theaters
- ❑ 14. Haunted Hotels
- ❑ 15. Ghosts, Werewolves, Witches and Vampires
- ❑ 16. Campfire Ghost Stories
- ❑ 17. Halloween Recipes and Crafts
- ❑ 18. Ghost Stories of America Volume I
- ❑ 19. Ontario Ghost Stories Volume II
- ❑ 20. Ghost Stories of Oregon
- ❑ 21. Ghost Stories of Pennsylvania

- 22. Ghost Stories of the Maritimes Volume II
- 23. Ghost Stories of America Volume II
- 24. Haunted Houses
- 25. Haunted Highways
- 26. Ghost Stories of New England
- 27. Ghost Stories of the Rocky Mountains Volume II
- 28. Ghost Stories of the Old West
- 29. Ghost Stories of the Old South
- 30. Haunted Schools
- 31. Ghost Stories of Pets and Animals
- 32. Ghost Stories of the Civil War
- 33. Canadian Ghost Stories Volume II
- 34. Haunted Halloween Stories
- 36. Ghost Stories of the Sea
- 37. Fireside Ghost Stories
- 39. Pumpkin Carving
- 40. Haunted Battlefields
- 41. Romantic Ghost Stories
- 42. Victorian Ghost Stories
- 43. Ghost Stories of New York State
- 44. Campfire Ghost Stories Volume II
- 45. Urban Legends
- 46. Ghost Stories of London
- 47. Werewolves and Shapeshifters
- 48. Haunted Cemeteries
- 49. Guardian Angels
- 50. Premonitions and Psychic Warnings
- 51. Gothic Ghost Stories
- 52. Scary Stories
- 53. Ghost Hunters
- 55. Famous People of the Paranormal
- 57. Haunting Fireside Stories
- 58. Scary Movies
- 60. Ghost Hunters of America

More Ghost House books will be available in the months ahead. Check with your local bookseller or order direct. U.S. readers call 1-800-518-3541. In Canada, call 1-800-661-9017.

www.lonepinepublishing.com